The Black Archive #32

THE ROMANS

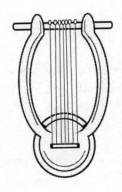

By Jacob Edwards

Published June 2019 by Obverse Books

Cover Design © Cody Schell

Text © Jacob Edwards, 2019

Range Editors: Paul Simpson, Philip Purser-Hallard

Jacob would like to thank all the good folk at the Black Archive,
especially Paul Simpson for his astute edits.

To Mum and Dad, for encouraging me in everything I do.

Also available

#1: *Rose* by Jon Arnold

#2: *The Massacre* by James Cooray Smith

#3: *The Ambassadors of Death* by LM Myles

#4: *Dark Water / Death in Heaven* by Philip Purser-Hallard

#5: *Image of the Fendahl* by Simon Bucher-Jones

#6: *Ghost Light* by Jonathan Dennis

#7: *The Mind Robber* by Andrew Hickey

#8: *Black Orchid* by Ian Millsted

#9: *The God Complex* by Paul Driscoll

#10: *Scream of the Shalka* by Jon Arnold

#11: *The Evil of the Daleks* by Simon Guerrier

#12: *Pyramids of Mars* by Kate Orman

#13: *Human Nature / The Family of Blood* by Philip Purser-Hallard
  and Naomi Jacobs

#14: *The Ultimate Foe* by James Cooray Smith

#15: *Full Circle* by John Toon

#16: *Carnival of Monsters* by Ian Potter

#17: *The Impossible Planet / The Satan Pit* by Simon Bucher-Jones

#18: *Marco Polo* by Dene October

#19: *The Eleventh Hour* by Jon Arnold

#20: *Face the Raven* by Sarah Groenewegen

#21: *Heaven Sent* by Kara Dennison

#22: *Hell Bent* by Alyssa Franke

#23: *The Curse of Fenric* by Una McCormack

#24: *The Time Warrior* by Matthew Kilburn

#25: *Doctor Who (1996)* by Paul Driscoll

#26: *The Dæmons* by Matt Barber

#27: *The Face of Evil* by Thomas Rodebaugh

#28: *Love & Monsters* by Niki Haringsma

#29: *The Impossible Astronaut / Day of the Moon* by John Toon

#30: *The Dalek Invasion of Earth* by Jonathan Morris

#31: *Warriors' Gate* by Frank Collins

CONTENTS

Overview

Synopsis

Introduction

Chapter 1: Why Comedy?

Chapter 2: Humour in *The Romans* – Is It Funny?

Chapter 3: Comedy After *The Romans*

Chapter 4: What Else Was New in *The Romans*?

Chapter 5: What Is History?

Chapter 6: Where Did *The Romans* Come From?

Chapter 7: How Historically Accurate Is *The Romans*?

Chapter 8: *The Romans* and Counter-Culture

Chapter 9: A Viewer's Response to *The Romans*

Bibliography

Acknowledgements

Biography

OVERVIEW

Serial Title: *The Romans*

Writer: Dennis Spooner

Director: Christopher Barry

Original UK Transmission Dates: 16 January 1965 – 6 February 1965

Running Time: 'The Slave Traders': 24m 14s

'All Roads Lead to Rome': 23m 14s

'Conspiracy': 26m 18s

'Inferno': 23m 09s

UK Viewing Figures: 'The Slave Traders': 13.0 million

'All Roads Lead to Rome': 11.5 million

'Conspiracy': 10.0 million

'Inferno': 12.0 million

Regular Cast: William Hartnell (Dr Who), William Russell (Ian Chesterton), Jacqueline Hill (Barbara Wright), Maureen O'Brien (Vicki)

Guest Cast: Derek Sydney (Sevcheria), Nicholas Evans (Didius), Dennis Edwards (Centurion), Margot Thomas (Stallholder), Edward Kelsey (Slave Buyer), Bart Allison (Maximus Pettulian), Barry Jackson (Ascaris), Peter Diamond (Delos), Michael Peake (Tavius), Dorothy-Rose Gribble (Woman Slave), Gertan Klauber (Galley Master), Ernest Jennings, John Caesar (Men in Market), Tony Lambden (Court Messenger), Derek Francis (Nero), Brian Proudfoot (Tigilinus), Kay Patrick (Poppaea), Anne Tirard (Locusta)

Antagonists: Nero, Sevcheria

Novelisation: *Doctor Who: The Romans* by Donald Cotton. **The Target Doctor Who Library** #120.

Responses:

'...a bold attempt to see just how far they could go with **Doctor Who** ... and what they could really expect to get away with. With *The Romans* they came dangerously close to breaking-point...'

[Paul Mount, 'Story Review', *Doctor Who: An Adventure in Space and Time* #M: *The Romans*]

'...Spooner, incoming story editor and genius writer of *The Romans*, gives the format one final tweak by allowing the Doctor to be cleverer, funnier, cooler – turning him into a hero we could cheer.'

[Gary Gillatt, *'The Rescue* and *The Romans'*, *Doctor Who Magazine* #406.]

SYNOPSIS

'The Slave Traders'

64 CE: a month after the TARDIS topples down a mountainside near Rome, **the Doctor**, **Ian**, **Barbara** and **Vicki** are enjoying life in a country villa. Barbara and Vicki visit a local market and are noticed by slave traders **Sevcheria** and **Didius**, who learn where they live. The Doctor decides to visit Rome, taking Vicki with him. That night, Sevcheria and Didius raid the villa, and capture Ian and Barbara.

On their way to Rome, the Doctor and Vicki find the body of a lyre player, **Maximus Pettulian**, for whom a Roman **centurion** mistakes the Doctor. Pettulian is expected at **Caesar Nero**'s court, and the Doctor accepts the offer of an escort to Rome.

Ian is sold as a galley slave and led off, much to Barbara's dismay.

The centurion orders a mute assassin, **Ascaris**, to kill 'Pettulian'.

'All Roads Lead to Rome'

The Doctor and Vicki see off Ascaris, who then hurls himself from the Doctor's window; the centurion also vanishes but the Doctor decides to continue to Rome. Unbeknownst to him and Vicki, Barbara is already there, and is bought by **Tavius**, who takes her to Nero's court to be an attendant for the emperor's wife, **Poppaea**.

Ian, meanwhile, is rowing on board a galley, but this ship is caught in a storm and he and another slave, **Delos**, are shipwrecked. They too head for Rome, where they are captured.

Arriving in Rome, Vicki and the Doctor just miss seeing Barbara at the slave auction. They proceed to Nero's court, where the Doctor, still posing as Maximus Pettulian, uses his wits to avoid having to perform for the emperor. Tavius directs the Doctor and Vicki to the apodyterium, where they find the missing centurion, dead.

Ian and Delos, now locked up in Barbara's old cell, are informed by Sevcheria they are to fight in the arena – against lions.

'Conspiracy'

In a furtive encounter, Tavius tells the Doctor he has disposed of the centurion's body, and urges him to delay his action.

Barbara attracts Nero's unwanted attention, and he chases her through the palace, eventually ending up in Poppaea's quarters. Nero maintains to his wife that it was Barbara chasing him. Poppaea goes to the court poisoner, **Locusta**, not knowing that Vicki has accidentally entered Locusta's rooms and is hiding there. When both women have gone, Vicki switches around two goblets of wine – one poisoned, one not.

Nero's servant **Tigilinus** arrives with the two goblets; Barbara drinks from one, before the Doctor rushes in to prevent Nero drinking from the other. Nero gives the goblet instead to Tigilinus, who drinks and dies.

At a banquet that evening, the Doctor 'plays' the lyre but first claims that only the most perceptive will be able to hear his music. Everyone at court is then wildly enthusiastic about his playing, except for Nero, who is furious and storms out. At the gladiatorial school, accompanied by a reluctant Barbara, Nero gloats to Sevcheria that Maximus' next audience will be in the arena – with the lions set on him mid-performance.

At Nero's behest, Ian and Delos are made to fight to the death.

Delos gains the upper hand and Nero commands him to cut off Ian's head.

'Inferno'

Delos tries instead to kill Nero, but fails, and, at Barbara's plea, he and Ian run for their lives. Nero believes they will return for Barbara, so has guards posted around the palace walls.

Poppaea orders Tavius to get rid of Barbara, but Barbara appeals to him for help, and warns him of Nero's plans for Maximus Pettulian. Tavius passes this information to the Doctor, and tells him it is time to act – Maximus Pettulian is in fact an assassin sent to kill Nero. After Tavius leaves, Nero and the Doctor bandy words about Maximus' impending fate, during which exchange the Doctor accidentally sets fires to Nero's blueprints for a New Rome. This gives Nero an idea...

Ian sneaks back into the palace with Delos, and Tavius reunites him with Barbara. Fingering a small cross he wears round his neck, Tavius watches them escape. The Doctor and Vicki also depart. While Rome burns, the Doctor claims he's not responsible for giving Nero the idea. Eventually, though, he finds the notion amusing.

Ian and Barbara reach the villa first, and greet the returning Doctor and Vicki, neither group realising how close or how often they came to crossing paths in Rome. They leave in the TARDIS, but some force starts to drag the Ship down...

INTRODUCTION

Doctor Who in its early years was a phoenix: each episode flared briefly and was gone, its successor emerging a week later from the ashes of a cliffhanger. The programme lived on but the stories themselves were never meant to last.

In the 1960s, television creation and consumption were by nature ephemeral. No-one intended **Doctor Who** – or any other show – to have rewatch value[1]. There were no DVDs or Blu-rays, and certainly nothing like video on demand. If you missed something, chances were you'd missed it forever[2].

It was only belatedly, with the advent of VHS and the ongoing popularity of **Doctor Who** in the 1970s, that fan culture sought out the show's early black-and-white stories and found a lamentable number to have been purged from the BBC Archives. Thankfully, *The Romans* (1965) wasn't junked. It survives in its entirety upon the shelves and within the devices of collectors. From a modern perspective, however, in an age where television is made not only to be broadcast but also, perhaps even primarily, to be retailed, it is important to remember the serial's origins.

The Romans, like all its kin, was one of hundreds of television mayflies. It wasn't a big-budget production or ratings blockbuster. It

---

[1] Or at least, very few people. We can only doff our caps to those who taped the broadcasts direct from TV to audio cassette.

[2] As **Doctor Who** was broadcast just before six o'clock on a Saturday evening, and Saturdays were often spent on location filming for future episodes, it wasn't uncommon for **Who** actors never to have seen themselves in the finished product.

was never intended to withstand ongoing scrutiny. Yet, this is what **The Black Archive** brings: scrutiny beyond proportion; an in-depth analysis of a programme made – in this case – more than five decades ago and only meant to be watched once.

Yes, half a century later, we're singling out four episodes of disposable television and passing judgement on them as if they comprised the 50th anniversary special. Ipso facto, we expect too much.

Still, *The Romans* stands up.

Despite its humble origins, despite the advances in television and the heights to which **Doctor Who** has soared, this old four-parter from 1965 remains a very good watch; on the one hand an important serial in the programme's history, while on the other just a funny, well-crafted piece of television. As we shall see, it was a departure from what **Doctor Who** had offered to that point. It introduced comedy and made several other, less immediately noticeable contributions to the show's ongoing development. Of the original run, it is, to my mind, one of few **Doctor Who** stories that genuinely repays a repeat screening, even for casual fans.

The current work will assess *The Romans* first as a comedy, secondly as an agent of change within **Doctor Who**, thirdly as history (in several different senses), and finally as a self-contained viewing experience. At the risk of spoilers, suffice here to say that it proves worthy.

Rome, it is oft said, wasn't built in a day. *The Romans* more or less **was**, yet still its fire burns.

CHAPTER 1: WHY COMEDY?

Time being the inexorable linear crawl that we know outside of fiction, the truth is that very few of **Doctor Who**'s fans nowadays were alive and tuning in when the programme was first broadcast. For viewers weaned on 21st-century **Who**'s fast-paced verbal badinage, the old black-and-white serials and tiny cathode ray tube TVs of the 1960s lie far beyond comprehension. How then can we hope to view a production like *The Romans* with any sort of perspective?

When **Doctor Who** was in the planning stages, children's writer Cecil Edwin Webber offered several fanciful suggestions:

> 'Or to think about Christmas: which seasonable story shall we take our characters into? Bethlehem? Was it by means of Dr Who's machine that Aladdin's palace sailed through the air? Was Merlin Dr Who? Was Cinderella's Godmother Dr Who's wife chasing him through time? Jacob Marley was Dr Who slightly tipsy, but what other tricks did he get up to that Yuletide?'[3]

The notion of the Doctor as Merlin did indeed surface years later in the Sylvester McCoy story *Battlefield* (1989), while several other of Webber's ideas seem as if they could have slipped back in time from a brainstorming session with 21st-century showrunner Steven Moffat. In 1963, however, Head of Drama Sydney Newman declared himself unimpressed by Webber's thoughts, and scribbled a contrary vision for how **Doctor Who** should develop:

---

[3] ''Dr Who' – General Notes on Background and Approach'.

'I don't like this much – it all reads silly **and condescending**. It doesn't get across the basis of teaching of educational experience – drama based upon and stemming from factual material and scientific phenomena and actual social history of past and future.'[4]

Newman conceptualised **Doctor Who** as a serious programme, and this at first is what eventuated. From the opening titles on 23 November 1963, through 53 weekly instalments and approximately 21 hours of screen time leading up to 'The Slave Traders' (episode 1 of *The Romans*) on 16 January 1965, the Doctor and his companions endured a procession of harrowing adventures offering barely a chuckle. Dennis Spooner, to be fair, wrote a comedy character for *The Reign of Terror* (1964), and other serials did have snatches of humour. These, however, were rare exceptions. **Doctor Who** as a rule was enthralling, thrilling, terrifying, and wondrous. It was an edifying (if surprisingly adult) ordeal through time and space. For example, in 'The Snows of Terror' (episode 4 of *The Keys of Marinus*, (1964)), Barbara is very nearly raped. This episode was broadcast just three days before the first public meeting of Mary Whitehouse's Clean Up TV Campaign (5 May 1964), during which Mrs Patricia Duce reported on the committee's first systematic vetting of prime time television for such objectionable content as sexual innuendo, unseemly dress, cruelty, sadism, violence, unrepentant malfeasance, and unnecessarily disturbing or dismal scenes. Although **Doctor Who** was culpable in respect to many of these, prime time was defined as the five-hour period between six and eleven o'clock at night. **Doctor Who**'s first season went out

---

[4] '"Dr Who" – General Notes on Background and Approach'.

between 5.15 and 6.00 and thus did not fall under 'adult' jurisdiction to be judged and condemned[5]. What it **wasn't**, in particular, however, was funny.

Why, then, the sudden and extraordinary departure?

The obvious answer is that David Whitaker, who was Script Editor from the show's outset through to *The Dalek Invasion of Earth* (1964), had left and been replaced by Spooner, a man of more comedic inclinations[6]. There may be a superficial truth in this. However, there is also evidence to suggest that the recourse to humour was far from capricious.

Spooner wrote:

> 'Certainly it was my intention to introduce a little light-heartedness into the plot. At that period of its history, each **Doctor Who** story was three hours long – six half-hour episodes – and this inevitably presented the script-writer with problems in episode 2. For at this point you don't want to get too much further into the story with things that should happen in episode 4. So humour is the answer. If you can introduce an element of humour through a specific character then it becomes a marvellous way of padding the programme without actually boring the audience or

[5] Thompson, Ben, ed, *Ban this Filth!*, pp61-66. Howe, David J, and Stephen James Walker, *The Television Companion: The Unofficial and Unauthorised Guide to Doctor Who, Volume One*, pp26-69)
[6] Spooner began his career writing material for stand-up comedians. For more information, see Morris, Jonathan: *The Black Archive #30: The Dalek Invasion of Earth.*

breaking up the plot!'[7]

Humour, then, was a tool; a means by which Spooner believed he could improve the writing. But in *The Reign of Terror* this manifested in just one minor character. *The Romans* was to be an entire serial devoted to humour. By what rationale could this be justified?

Again, Spooner:

> '*The Romans*, which I wrote for the second season of the series, was more of a deliberate attempt to see how far we could go in doing a comedy **Doctor Who**. It was almost *A Funny Thing Happened to the Doctor on the Way to the Forum* story![8] What had happened by then was that we had realised the show was now destined to run for a long time. And in television you have to learn very quickly what you are going to get away with, because once a series becomes at all established then you cannot change it.'[9]

In essence, **Doctor Who** had proven a bigger hit than anyone anticipated[10]; having survived its first year, the show had to start

---

[7] Spooner, Dennis, 'The Secret of Writing for **Doctor Who**', in Haining, Peter, *The Doctor Who File*, p74.

[8] *A Funny Thing Happened on the Way to the Forum* was a Broadway musical. It premiered in 1962, and from 1963 ran in London's West End. A film version was made in 1966, subsequent to *The Romans*.

[9] Spooner, 'The Secret of Writing for **Doctor Who**', p74.

[10] Whitaker, for instance, says he moved on in part because, unsure of **Doctor Who**'s future, he had secured a job with a different production ('David Whitaker (1970s)').

preparing itself for longevity. There would be cast changes to deal with and a Catch-22 entwinement with the Daleks. Eventually the Doctor himself would regenerate. While nobody at the time could have anticipated just how long-lived **Doctor Who** would become – or how big a role humour would play in its scripts – Spooner for one already was contemplating the question of how the programme could stay fresh yet familiar throughout its continuing success.

Spooner sought to test the limits. He followed *The Romans* with *The Web Planet* (1965), which was a conscious foray to the far, bizarre edges of SF and a means by which to assay the BBC's technical capabilities[11]. Fair to say, *The Web Planet* comes across as one of **Doctor Who**'s great failed experiments; but in *The Romans*, at least, Spooner struck out successfully in a direction that **Doctor Who** could – and perhaps needed to – explore further.

Doctor Who was ostensibly an adventure serial. It allowed viewers to experience history and speculate about the future. However, the conceit by which this was achieved – two schoolteachers abducted by an old man in a malfunctioning time machine – brought with it a perhaps unintended corollary; namely, a growing sense of despair and, for want of a better term, battle fatigue.

There is no triumph in the time travellers' adventures; merely survival. Ian and Barbara do their best to find wonder in their surroundings, but, unlike those of the derring-do heroes of other weekly serials, their escapades for the most part form a litany of plights from which they cannot escape. Week after week, planet after planet, and time period after time period, they find

---

[11] Spooner, 'The Secret of Writing for **Doctor Who**', p74.

themselves adrift and attacked, captured, coerced, fearful for their lives. Any catalogue of their travails would make for grim reading, but suffice here to say that Ian is knocked unconscious a lot and Barbara, upon parting ways with the Doctor, shapes as a prime candidate for posttraumatic stress disorder.

The early **Doctor Who** stories, in short, took to heart Sydney Newman's emphasis on realism and adventure, contriving to present not only situations of genuine distress but also a veritable barrage of blunt instrument clubbings[12], throttlings, shootings, stabbings, and screaming, gut-wrenching onscreen death. The first three serials offered nothing at all to mitigate this trauma – no hint of respite – and it was only with 'Five Hundred Eyes' (episode 3 of *Marco Polo*, 1964) that the character of the Doctor was softened a little, and that moments of levity started to be written into the scripts. Even then, **Doctor Who** was rarely intentionally funny. But there was, at least, some nascent recognition of what was needed.

Doctor Who prior to Dennis Spooner's arrival wasn't always scary, but it **was** bleak. Moreover, it offered bleakness without respite. By the time Terry Nation and director Richard Martin conjured up a forsaken London for the Daleks to terrorise in *The Dalek Invasion of Earth*[13], one senses that the year-long build-up of doom and gloom was reaching dangerous levels. Over-focussed by its mandate for

---

[12] A far, strangled cry from the reaction shots of 21st-century **Who**, or indeed those genteel Pertwee-era karate chops to the shoulder.
[13] Truly a desolate, dismal adventure, rife with violence. *Resurrection of the Daleks* (1984) would furnish the programme with its highest ever body-count, yet this seems almost a natural progression from the carnage being flung about the place 20 years earlier by Nation and Martin.

drama, what **Doctor Who** lacked was a relief valve. Instinctively — and with differing levels of finesse — some writers and directors had indeed cast an eye to humour, but nothing was formalised. What laughs there were seem uncertain; illicit, almost.

Enter, Dennis Spooner, sounding the imperial raspberry and splashing merrily in a watershed moment of history...

Cue *The Romans*!

CHAPTER 2: HUMOUR IN *THE ROMANS* – IS IT FUNNY?

Although this question demands a one-word answer – yes! – the long history of **Doctor Who** does makes an assessment somewhat problematic, as does the fact that **Doctor Who** in the 1960s was sold to many Commonwealth countries, and today is viewed in more parts of the world than ever. A deeper appreciation of cultural predilections and peculiarities vis-à-vis humour lies – sadly – outside the scope of this chapter. For the purposes of evaluating *The Romans*, we shall limit ourselves to a British baseline (as interpreted by an Australian).

So, was *The Romans* funny when first shown? Is it funny compared to 21st-century **Who**? Will it be funny years from now? Tastes vary from person to person, and change over time. What follows is an attempt to contextualise *The Romans'* humour within the distinct comedic zeitgeists of those years when the serial saw official release.

Humour in 1965 – The Original Broadcast

From an inspection of the BBC's Audience Research Report, **Doctor Who** historians David J Howe and Stephen James Walker testify that the majority of those viewers sampled in 1965 took issue with the final episode of *The Romans*[14]. The programme was dismissed as farcical, violent and unrealistic. Each of these criticisms deserves our attention.

---

[14] Howe and Walker, *The Television Companion, Volume One*, pp92-93.

- **Farce:** Although 'Conspiracy' (episode 3 of *The Romans*) contains most of the overt farce, 'Inferno' (episode 4) does also have its moments. Farce, however, was neither unknown nor unloved in Britain at the time. From 1958 to 1964 there had been 10 films made in the **Carry On** franchise[15]; television audiences had groped at, grasped and come to grips with **The Benny Hill Show** (1955-67)[16]; and the aforementioned Broadway musical farce *A Funny Thing Happened on the Way to the Forum* had enjoyed a highly successful run in London. Curated reproofs of *The Romans* notwithstanding, in 1965 farce was in vogue.

- **Violence:** Allegations that *The Romans* might be too violent are, if not themselves farcical, then at least not without a certain absurdity. What programme did these people think they'd been watching? In absolute terms *The Romans* was

---

[15] **Carry On** offered a relentless barrage of slapstick, innuendo and naughty postcard titillation. Subsequent to *The Romans* it churned out at least one additional title per year up until 1978. William Hartnell starred in the very first **Carry On** film, *Carry On Sergeant* (1958), and both Derek Sydney (Sevcheria) and Gertan Klauber (Galley Master) had appeared more recently in *Carry On Spying* (1964), and in Klauber's case also *Carry on Cleo* (1964). Derek Francis himself would later become associated with **Carry On**, to such an extent that 21st-century viewers sometimes assume he was cast in **Doctor Who** as a result and thus played Nero in the **Carry On** style. (For instance, John West in 'Land of Make Believe', #27 of the **I'll Explain Later** podcast, describes Francis as 'a stalwart of the **Carry On** era'... which Francis was, but not when he played Nero.)

[16] Albeit not yet the full-blown 'Yakety Sax' incarnation of the programme; this would emerge in colour under the same name from 1969-89.

less violent than most of **Doctor Who**'s stories to that date. What set it apart, perhaps, was the comedic association. In other words, those concerned with propriety judged it acceptable for people to be strangled, stabbed, clubbed, shot, and blown up in great numbers before 6pm on a Saturday evening, but not for the Doctor to drop puns referencing Nero's plan to feed him to the lions.

- **Realism:** Again, this seems an odd quibble. **Doctor Who** premised itself around a time-travelling police box, and in the first two stories of the second season had, respectively, shrunk its protagonists to matchstick size and dunked Daleks in the Thames. One could argue that the historical episodes had been more measured in content, yet even these – most recently *The Reign of Terror* – were hardly paragons of accuracy or believability. What seems likely to have irked critics of *The Romans* is the lack of **tonal** realism – the fact that the Doctor is uncharacteristically carefree, and that Nero is played for laughs. The past, then, was something that **Doctor Who** had taken seriously, but now wasn't.

All three gripes amount to much the same thing: *The Romans* didn't offer up what viewers were used to. Any naysaying in the BBC's Audience Research Report is in this sense reflexive, and we ought tip our hats to Dennis Spooner for having had the foresight to test the waters and, if not inure **Doctor Who**'s audience to comedy, then at least make the first overtures. In sporting parlance, *The Romans* took one for the team. It sacrificed its own standing for the future good of the programme.

As Tat Wood and Lawrence Miles have noted, 'Conspiracy' – the instalment with the overt run-around farce – was broadcast on the same day as former Prime Minister Winston Churchill's state funeral[17]. This was an unfortunate piece of timing. BBC One – before proceeding to its usual Saturday afternoon fare of **Grandstand** (1958-2007), **Juke Box Jury** (1959-67), and **Doctor Who** – devoted five hours to valedictory programming and a live telecast of the funeral procession and service[18]. Churchill had proven an inspirational leader and orator throughout the Second World War, and with this conflict still a relatively recent memory in 1965, the scale of British mourning should not be underestimated. By late afternoon some people may have appreciated a let-up such as *The Romans* offered, but little wonder if many more were in no mood to see famous historical figures prancing about in the **Carry On** style.

We should bear in mind, too, that the farce of 'Conspiracy', though no doubt influencing viewers' overall assessment of *The Romans*, was a far cry in (lack of) subtlety from the humour of the other episodes. On 23 January 1965 – subsequent to 'The Slave Traders' but prior to 'All Roads Lead to Rome' (*The Romans* episode 2), Churchill's death and then the farce of 'Conspiracy' – a reviewer from *The Times* expressed approval of the programme, noting what seems a qualitative parity between **Doctor Who** and what he or she saw as the 'disarming blend of fact, fantasy and beat music' offered by Rediffusion's children's variety programme **Ollie and Fred's Five O'Clock Club** (1963-66):

'The strongest weapon in the BBC armoury, by contrast,

---

[17] Wood, Tat and Lawrence Miles, *About Time 1: The Unauthorized Guide to Doctor Who, 1963-1966, Seasons 1 to 3*, p129.
[18] BBC Genome Project: Radio Times 1923-2009.

remains [**Doctor Who**]: the departure of the Daleks has broken small hearts all over the country, but the new series, with Miss Jacqueline Hill and Mr William Russell in the hands of the slave traders, promises well. Miss Verity Lambert's production is once again flawless.'[19]

One notable aspect of this *Times* review is that its focus rests on the **content** of **Five O'Clock Club** but on the **delivery** of **Doctor Who**. It is not, thus, a like-for-like comparison. This does not detract from the positive but may serve to caution us in our drawing of genre parallels. In positioning *The Romans* alongside contemporary rib-ticklers such as *Carry On Cleo* and the original production of *A Funny Thing Happened on the Way to the Forum*, we should bear in mind that *Cleo* was a film comedy and *A Funny Thing* played out on stage. To appreciate *The Romans'* humour, we need recognise that it was not merely a comedy; it was a **television** comedy, broadcast in what was still at that time a burgeoning industry.

The first British TV licences were issued in 1947 but it wasn't until 1958 that any claim could be made that television had become commonplace[20]. British broadcast comedy during the 1950s belonged undisputedly to radio – in particular, **The Goon Show** (1951-60), which mixed wordplay with sound effects and general absurdity, lighting a torch of surrealness that would pass to television most famously by way of **Monty Python's Flying Circus**

---

[19] 'Keeping the Children Happy and Informed', *The Times*, 23 January 1965.
[20] One could buy a radio-only licence, or one that covered both TV and radio. 1958 was the year when the combined licence first outnumbered the radio-only (BBC Annual Reports).

(1969-74).

In these early days, the one programme that sat squarely on the crossroads between radio and television supremacy was **Hancock's Half Hour**, which lived a double life and proved immensely popular in both mediums (radio, 1955-59; television, 1956-61). It was **Hancock** that shifted the focus of humour from music-hall-styled variety shows like **Benny Hill** to character- and situation-based comedy:

> 'Much of the humour [...] springs from the audience being positioned in such a way that they can witness the clear disjuncture between [the character, Tony] Hancock's constant desire to better himself and the altogether sadder reality of his day-to-day existence.'[21]

The Romans is rightly referred to as a farce: Nero's pursuit of Barbara qualifies unequivocally; and there is also physical humour (the Doctor's fight scene), the inherent absurdity of a poisoner by appointment (Locusta), and the dramatic irony that's played up via repeated instances of the Doctor and Barbara almost but not quite crossing paths. Nonetheless, there are also more subtle elements of comedy: wordplay that harks back to the glory days of radio; and a remarkably **Hancock**-esque disparity between self-image and viewer perception. The comedy characters sit especially well in this light, and Nero most prominently of all. Granted, one anonymous voice from the BBC Audience Research Report complained of

---

[21] Kilborn, Richard, 'A Golden Age of British Sitcom? **Hancock's Half Hour** and **Steptoe and Son**', in Kamm, Juergen, and Birgit Neumann, eds, *British TV Comedies: Cultural Concepts, Contexts and Controversies*, p25.

'Inferno' (episode 4): 'This programme gets more and more bizarre; in fact it's so ridiculous it's a bore!'[22]

But 'Inferno' is *The Romans'* sombre denouement. It sees Rome burn while a deranged Nero laughs and plays his lyre. Bizarre? Ridiculous? From a historical perspective, yes; and yet, this is the natural endpoint for a character who sees himself as divinely imbued and aloof from the world, set apart by his music. It isn't just a throwaway nod to historical events; it is the tipping point where an archetypal **Hancock** character's delusions of grandeur grow beyond the point where even the most practised of self-deceptions can contain them[23].

Where *The Romans* differed from **Hancock's Half Hour** and the other comedy heavyweight of the time, **Steptoe and Son** (1962-65, 1970-74)[24], was in its doubling down on the humour of social mobility. The younger Steptoe and Hancock both aspire – and fail – to rise above the lowly stations of their birth, but in *The Romans* it is Nero (and to a lesser extent, the Doctor) who longs to elevate himself. Let's emphasise that: Nero, ruler of the Roman Empire! His ineffectual pursuit of refinement – exemplified by music that is never played; undercut by his own low self-esteem and base actions – lends an odd slant to the comedy of class. Elevation, in fact, is not the right word. Nero is floundering, trying unconvincingly to stay

---

[22] Quoted in Howe and Walker, *The Television Companion* volume 1, p92.

[23] In terms of function, it calls to mind Major Kong's hollering exit astride the bomb that will end everything in *Dr Strangelove* (1964).

[24] In addition to its one-off nature and the absence of a laughter track, neither of which are insignificant (Kilborn, 'A Golden Age of British Sitcom?' pp26, 32).

afloat. He doesn't seek upward mobility so much as a pair of armbands to keep from sinking.

The Romans, in short, called upon humorous elements that were well-recognised in successful British comedies of the era. The heightened take on social mobility — having the aspiring character being not of low- but of the highest birth — was perhaps too great a liberty for a children's drama programme (with an established history) to take and get away with in a single story; but this notwithstanding, *The Romans* was, by objective contemporary standards, funny. That it was underappreciated surely owes more to audience expectations than to its intrinsic quality.

Humour in 1987 – *The Romans* Novelisation

A long time passed between *The Romans'* original screening and its eventual appearance in print. Spooner himself had died in 1986, and the task of novelising his script fell to Donald Cotton. *The Romans* was published the following year, midway between the end of season 23 (Colin Baker's last) and the beginning of season 24 (Sylvester McCoy's first). **Doctor Who** by this point had drifted far from its origins, as had British television comedy.

The Romans on TV may have been a radical departure for **Doctor Who**, but at the time was still relatively conservative in its humour. Subsequent to 1965, British TV exploded with a new wave of satirical, surreal, and downright anarchic comedies: **The Goodies** (1970-80); **The Hitchhiker's Guide to the Galaxy** (1981)[25]; **The Young Ones** (1982-84); **Blackadder** (1983-89); and many others.

---

[25] Although this was more successful in its earlier guise as a radio programme (1978-80).

Less ground-breaking sitcoms still had their place – witness the success of 'Allo 'Allo (1982-92) – but it is no great stretch to think that the much-altered comedic landscape would have given Donald Cotton pause when he came to revisiting Dennis Spooner's script.

To do justice to *The Romans*, Cotton needed to reproduce in written form a comedy that relied to a considerable extent on physical humour and nuances in performance. His approach to this task was one of liberal translation. He spurned a straight retelling, omitted all the onscreen dialogue, and instead presented the story by way of letters and journal entries (as written by various of the characters). The result is unquestionably one of the oddest books in the Target range. *The Romans* in metamorphosed form is funny, but in an entirely different way from its progenitor.

Firstly, it's **all** funny. Those plot points that were treated seriously by Spooner – Ian's stint as a galley slave, for instance, and his ceaseless concern for Barbara – are recounted much like all others: that is, in a tone of hapless befuddlement. Cotton's narrators all use more or less the same voice; and although each evinces the blithe self-centredness of the Hancock-type character, their respective dissociations from reality suggest a heightened manifestation thereof. The plot is no longer that of a comings-and-goings story with witty delivery; it is an almost surrealist piece of absurdism.

Secondly, *The Romans* as novelised is mostly the same **type** of funny. Where Spooner had employed farce and wordplay, and had allowed the actors room to enact bits of comic business, Cotton instead plumps mainly for the humour of character ineptitude and obliviousness[26]. To this end he takes considerable licence. The Doctor, for instance, doesn't narrowly avoid crossing paths with Barbara; he just **doesn't recognise her**:

> 'One of them, a really quite handsome but woebegone young woman, bore some slight resemblance to Barbara – although the latter, I am sure, would never have consented to appear in public in so dishevelled a condition! However, the similarity was sufficient to give me further cause for self-congratulation that I had had the wisdom to leave Miss Wright at the villa, where she can come to no possible harm. The slave-girl appeared to sense my interest, and waved at me frantically; but I nevertheless rejected Sevcheria's insulting invitation to make an offer for the poor woman.'[27]

Similarly, after his first confrontation with the assassin Ascaris, the Doctor through happy accident survives two further attempts on his life, neither of which was in Spooner's script[28]. Then, instead of fooling everyone with his Emperor's New Clothes routine, he deludes himself into thinking he can play the lyre. The story is not merely being told differently; it's an entirely different story.

Despite taking liberties (or perhaps because it did so?), Cotton's

---

[26] The novelisation does contain punning – it is, in fact, bursting with it – but Cotton's characters indulge not in the sharp, targeted repartee that Spooner favoured, but instead a stream-of-consciousness association that as often as not favours alliteration over genuine wordplay; the book contains some very funny lines but they are lost somewhat in the shuffle.

[27] Cotton, Donald, *Doctor Who: The Romans*, p47.

[28] Cotton, *The Romans*, pp64-65, 101-02.

novelisation of *The Romans* is – strangely, feverishly, irreverently, even inappropriately[29], but undeniably – funny; moreover, it is as strikingly original a contribution to the Target range as the TV serial had been to a programme not then known for anything but serious-minded drama[30]. Of all the roads that might have led from the black-and-white days of 1965 to a novelisation of *The Romans*, Cotton followed a trail of innovation that already had taken prospective readers through 20-plus on-screen years.

Humour in 1994 – *The Romans* on VHS

Seven years after Donald Cotton's novelisation, *The Romans* was released on video. Several more influential comedies had appeared during this time, including SF sitcom **Red Dwarf** (original run 1988-99) and the silent antics of **Mr Bean** (1990-95). The latter, with its man-child protagonist and reliance on physical humour, was something of a kindred spirit to *The Romans*. Viewers who took to Rowan Atkinson's rubber-faced expressiveness could reasonably be expected to have appreciated Derek Francis as Nero.

Nevertheless, nearly 30 years had passed since the original TV broadcast. The remainder of **Doctor Who** had come and gone, the show's original run ending in cancellation in 1989. Attempts had been made to stage an unofficial continuation but by 1994 all talk

---

[29] Alyson Fitch-Safreed in the **Doctor Who Target Book Club** podcast (#12 'The Romans') notes the unsettling effect of Cotton's making light of, for example, the burning of Christians – a historical atrocity not referenced in Spooner's script.

[30] Perhaps the need to have *The Romans* carry its original sense of innovation explains, in some measure, Cotton's recourse to the epistolary.

was of an impending US revival. **Doctor Who** was gone but coming back, bigger and better and (to many people's concern) American[31]. In this colourful fantasy world of big-name filmmakers and actors, what mark could *The Romans*, an old black-and-white serial, hope to make?

An important point to note here is that the audience had changed. Whereas *The Romans* in 1965 had been pitched at children (at least nominally) and criticised by their parents, the video release of 1994 targeted deep-pocketed **Doctor Who** fans; adults, in other words. Moreover, these were fans who a) were living in a state of withdrawal from their favourite programme, b) were effervescing about the prospect of new **Who**, and c) wouldn't, in most cases, ever have seen *The Romans*. In these circumstances a good number of viewers would have been predisposed to like what they saw.

Humour in 2008 – *The Romans* Audio Soundtrack

Fourteen years later, *The Romans* was released as a 'television soundtrack'. A soundtrack in this instance doesn't mean the incidental music; it refers to the serial as originally broadcast, only **without the picture**. Listening, in other words, to television. It's a medium that came as a godsend in the case of **Doctor Who**'s missing episodes; with the absence of visuals being mitigated by linking narration – in *The Romans*' case by Ian Russell – these original sound recordings often gave a far better sense of the lost stories than did the Target novelisations.

---

[31] For more on the Americanisation of **Who**, see Driscoll, Paul, *The Black Archive #25, Doctor Who (1996)*.

But for a story where the episodes all exist? One can only assume that a new generation of **Doctor Who** fans had arisen alongside the DVD, hungry for new-old material but without necessarily having ready access to VHS (the only legitimate way to watch the episodes at that point).

And this, of course, was the case.

The turn of the century shook out another wave of TV comedies, but their coming seems relatively unimportant compared to the changes in **Doctor Who** itself. In 1996 the American TV movie (and back-door pilot) *Doctor Who* failed to impress. More long years passed, during which Big Finish Productions (founded 1996) began putting out original **Doctor Who** audio adventures. **Doctor Who**'s 40th anniversary saw an ambitious webcast in the form of *Scream of the Shalka* (2003), but this was stillborn as an attempted BBC revival.

Finally, in 2005, **Doctor Who** was relaunched. It proved rather popular.

This, then, was the atmosphere in which *The Romans* audio soundtrack went on sale. **Doctor Who** was undergoing an unprecedented two-pronged resurgence. Fans both old and new were eager to delve deeper into the show's past. Whatever was being put out would be bought.

In this sense, the humorousness of *The Romans* in audio form is barely even of relevance. The soundtrack is, however, funny. William Russell's narration gives an excellent sense of what's going on – arguably, some of the physical scenes are even more effective this way – and the emphasis on dialogue allows for a greater appreciation of Spooner's script. *The Romans* as broadcast was a sharp mix of visual and spoken comedy; the audio soundtrack leans heavily towards the latter, but in doing so offers a subtle, quite charming variation.

Humour in 2009 – *The Romans* on DVD

The DVD of *The Romans* came out in February 2009, the gap year between Series 4 and Series 5 of the relaunched **Doctor Who**. This was a well-timed release, not only hawking the serial to a viewership starved of all but David Tennant's swansong specials but also pitching it on the heels of the Complete Fourth Series DVD and Blu-ray box sets. It is through two stories from Series 4 – with Catherine Tate as Donna Noble – that 21st-century **Who** resonates most closely with *The Romans*.

Episode 2 of the season, *The Fires of Pompeii* (2008), saw the Doctor and Donna arrive in Pompeii, 79 CE. This return to Roman times has more than just iconography to link it to the 1965 serial. There is also the 10th Doctor's throwaway admission of (at least partial) culpability in starting the Great Fire of Rome, and the fact that Donna, like Vicki, is making her first trip in the TARDIS. The serial, in fact, echoes *The Romans* in having as its focus the inviolability of history. Donna, like Vicki, wants to intervene (only more determinedly and without the teenager's whimsy). The subject receives a proper dramatic treatment, far from the frivolity of *The Romans*. Nonetheless, anyone watching the respective DVDs would be struck by the parallel.

Where *The Fires of Pompeii* recalled *The Romans* in subject matter, the preceding serial – episode 1 of Series 4, *Partners in Crime* (2008) – recaptured some of its tone. *Partners in Crime* begins with jaunty music and Donna walking along a crowded street. It cuts to the Doctor strolling hands-in-pockets in the other direction. These are characters who had met once in the 2006 Christmas special *The Runaway Bride* before going their separate ways. It looks now as if they'll cross paths again... but for 22 minutes they don't. Both are investigating Adipose Industries. Both pose as health and safety inspectors. Yet, in a well-staged sequence of close calls, they keep missing each other. The tone of events becomes more sinister. The music darkens, yet still carries a comedic undertone. Even once the Doctor and Donna do finally meet, the comedy continues.

Partners in Crime is an episode-long farce, making it by far a bigger and more sustained caper than episode 3 (or indeed all) of *The Romans*. Its reassociation of **Doctor Who** with the genre, along with *The Fire of Pompeii*'s harking back to the ancient setting, would have ensured that viewers of *The Romans* on DVD had the best possible context in which to appreciate the older serial's comedy[32]. Whether by chance or by design, *The Romans* in 2009 was brought into the fold and reaffirmed as funny.

Humour in 2019 (and Beyond)

At some point in the future we can expect an audiobook of Donald Cotton's novelisation. As with the original transfer of *The Romans* from TV to book, this will be a difficult undertaking. Whoever reads will have to handle several ostensibly disparate narrators, and

---

[32] See Aggas, James, '**Doctor Who** Retro Review: *The Romans* (First Doctor Story)' for an example of someone moving on from *The Fires of Pompeii* to watch and review *The Romans*: '*The Romans* still holds up as a really solid **Doctor Who** story. While some of the humour may be dated in some areas, it's still funny to watch at times.'

through inflection give voice to peculiarities that aren't especially evident on the page. If done well, the audiobook will be fantastic.

Conceivably, the early **Doctor Who** stories could be reimagined one day as graphic novels. The art would be serious and the tone predominantly dark... until *The Romans*, which would demand drawings by Didier Conrad (successor to Albert Uderzo) and function perfectly as an **Asterix**-style comic strip. Indeed, envisaging *The Romans* in this form is a good way to emphasise the comedic difference between it and the preceding serials.

Beyond that, the only basis for a new release of *The Romans* would be if the serial were to be colourised. Again, this would have to be done well, but there's no doubt it would cast the story – and thus the comedy – in a new light. Whereas black-and-white television seems intrinsically dated, *The Romans* remains, in essence, fresh and vital; a sumptuous dash of imperial colour would only add to its lustre.

Time, of course, will continue to pass, and *The Romans* (in audio, written, or its original visual form) will be discovered by new generations of **Who** fans. For the moment – 50-plus years after its small-screen debut, stacked against not only its 1960s contemporaries but also the serials of the '70s and '80s and then the fast-paced polish of 21st-century **Doctor Who** – *The Romans* is holding up well. For all that television has moved on, it remains funny.

As to the future, well, who can tell?

Ultimately any verdict on *The Romans*' humour must be subjective; yet, even those viewers who find it more historical than hysterical – more laborious than uproarious – should appreciate the intent.

Before *The Romans* there was nothing; then history proclaimed, 'Let there be laughter.'

Doctor Who hasn't looked back.

CHAPTER 3: COMEDY AFTER *THE ROMANS*

Far from merely dabbling with comedy, *The Romans* embraced it to the full, establishing not only precedents that echo through **Doctor Who**'s history but also benchmarks − high-water marks? − for saturation, diversity and overtness of humour. This section will outline *The Romans*' comedic legacy.

Immediate Aftermath (1965-66)

After *The Romans*, season 2 continued with three very serious stories − *The Web Planet*; then *The Crusade* and *The Space Museum* (both 1965) − before lightening up with *The Chase* (1965), a six-part Terry Nation runaround intended to make the Daleks more fun. The humour here is rather patchy, and none-too-subtle, the nadir coming atop the Empire State Building with Peter Purves' prolonged and cringeworthy appearance as sent-up hillbilly Morton Dill[33]. Purves later proved himself a fine actor, returning in 'The Planet of

---

[33] 'Flight Through Eternity' (*The Chase* episode 3). Dennis Spooner by this time was script-editing **Doctor Who**, and must bear some responsibility. In the audio commentary to 'Flight Through Eternity', director Richard Martin says of Dill's incredulous, irreverent inspection of a Dalek: 'That's a Dennis Spoonerism. Dennis invented this. It wasn't at all a Terry Nation thing.' But here we see a key difference between *The Romans* and *The Chase*. Spooner may have dictated a more comedic approach, and in the former case, with Christopher Barry's direction, was able to carry it through successfully; yet, humour was a tricky business, and the ham-fistedness with which Morton Dill was written (and directed; Martin heaps praise upon the performance) in large part bears the hallmarks of Terry Nation.

Decision' (episode 6) as new companion Steven Taylor. As Dill, however, he was terribly ill-used.

The next piece of **Doctor Who** comedy followed directly on from *The Chase*, and was written by Dennis Spooner himself. This was *The Time Meddler* (1965), a mostly sober story that nevertheless featured one of **Who**'s more memorable characters: the irrepressibly impish Time Lord (as it was later revealed) the Meddling Monk, who played gramophone records in the year 1066 so as to impersonate an entire Saxon monastery, and whose plan was to change history by firing atomic bazookas at the invading Vikings. The humour rests in part upon Peter Butterworth's performance – which anticipates the naughty schoolboy aspect of Patrick Troughton's Doctor – and in part on the fact that the Monk, for all that he is the villain, is not so unlike the Doctor (albeit more like the Doctor as he would become in future incarnations). Both are renegades; both tinker to change (in their own minds, improve) history. The Monk is less self-righteous, less moralistic about it, yet was it not the Doctor who accidentally gave spark to the fire of Rome, and who recently brought about the eerie tableau aboard the *Mary Celeste*? The Monk, in short, is who the Doctor could become were he to be more conscious an interventionist and less of an old fuddy-duddy[34].

Soon after *The Time Meddler* came *The Myth Makers* (1965), a sublime comedy that, perhaps most lamentably of all, falls amongst those episodes of **Doctor Who** that the BBC saw fit to junk. Visually, the serial is entirely lost, yet from its audio soundtrack alone – and

---

[34] Certainly, one suspects that the Monk wouldn't be out of place in 21st-century **Who**.

if not from that, then from Donald Cotton's absurdly droll novelisation of his own script – a quintessentially Spooner-ish comedy emerges. *The Myth Makers* satirises the Trojan War of Homer's *Iliad*, playing on audience expectations as the Doctor, despite earlier having scoffed at the notion, is tasked with infiltrating Troy and is forced at the last to pre-invent the Trojan Horse. As with *The Romans*, the comedy plays hand-in-hand with serious issues and actual history (however hazily it has come to us via myth-like storytelling).

Shortly after *The Myth Makers*, Cotton attempted something similar with *The Gunfighters* (1966), a comic take as much on widely held tropes of the American Wild West as on the Gunfight at the OK Corral specifically. *The Gunfighters* was to be less clear-cut a triumph, but nevertheless makes a worthy third instalment in **Doctor Who**'s first and best comedic trilogy.

In the years 1965-66, spanning seasons 2 and 3 of **Doctor Who**, comedy was employed both often and deliberately to counterbalance the more downbeat drama. This is no more evident than in 'The Feast of Steven' and 'Volcano', which fell respectively on Christmas Day 1965 and New Year's Day 1966, and were the seventh and eighth episodes of the otherwise rather grim 12-part epic *The Daleks' Master Plan* (1965-66). In 'The Feast of Steven', the TARDIS arrives on a film set, and the Doctor and company become embroiled in the silent comedy escapades of such notables as Charlie Chaplin and the Keystone Cops[35]. In 'Volcano', the TARDIS materialises first in the middle of a cricket match, then in Trafalgar

---

[35] Again, the episode has been junked, leaving us with silent comedy on an audio soundtrack only; a curious arrangement.

Square during New Year festivities. These interruptions to the main plot of *The Daleks' Master Plan* seem particularly glaring when the serial is experienced all at once, but at time of broadcast could, in theory, have provided some considerable relief. The fact that they **didn't** is not the point[36]. 'The Feast of Steven' and 'Volcano' were **Doctor Who**'s first holiday specials, an aspect of the programme that has returned, much-loved, in the 21st century and which owes its origins to the comedic leeway afforded by *The Romans*.

Regeneration and Character-Based Humour: A Decade of Dearth (1967-77)

Subsequent to Dennis Spooner and Donald Cotton's comedy blitzkrieg of 1965-66, **Doctor Who** took an extended break from whole-story humour.

Patrick Troughton began his tenure with a penchant for silly hats, and forged an oft-comical dynamic with Frazer Hines (playing Jamie McCrimmon)[37]. The odd funny moment aside, however, Troughton's serials carried a distinct aura of claustrophobic peril and suspense. The dourness of this era appears at first a reaction against overt comedy à la *The Romans*. In truth, though, it merely took the same problem – the week-by-week attrition of viewers' nerves – and solved it in a different way. Instead of the occasional big pressure

---

[36] As per Howe and Walker's study of the BBC's Audience Research Report (Howe and Walker, *The Television Companion* volume 1 p148), half the viewers surveyed were less than taken with 'The Feast of Steven'.

[37] To illustrate, there is a lovely scene in *The Tomb of the Cybermen* episode 1 (1967) where the Doctor accidentally takes Jamie's hand instead of Victoria's while stepping across the threshold.

release, Troughton's stories came with a built-in valve (the Doctor himself, plus Jamie), which kept the subject matter from becoming too oppressive.

When Jon Pertwee took on the lead role in 1970, **Doctor Who** underwent a sea change that for several seasons rendered it mostly Earthbound. In addition to this shift in setting – the familiarity of which would be proof against overwrought imaginations[38] – the programme's run was cut from 40-plus to 25 weekly episodes per season. Where previously the parade of dangers had proven gruelling in its ubiquity, now it could be savoured from behind the proverbial sofa and then put aside (leading to craving and anticipation) for half a year. The need for humour was gone, and what little remained in the Pertwee era became increasingly associated with the bemusement of UNIT personnel, and with the Brigadier's sardonic quips.

Which brings us to Tom Baker. The fourth Doctor spent his first four seasons (1974-78) immersed in so-called gothic horror (with the occasional piece of dark satire care of Script Editor Robert Holmes). This was **Doctor Who** at its most uncompromising, and unlike the early Hartnell episodes with their litany of chokings and bludgeonings, mid-70s **Who** fell to the censorious attention of outspoken moral campaigner Mary Whitehouse. The result was another sea change – this one prescribed from on high – and a

---

[38] Even if Pertwee himself took the opposite view: 'I always feel there's nothing more alarming than coming home to find a Yeti in your bathroom! OK, you might expect that in the Himalayas, but not in the average suburb.' (Pertwee, Jon, 'A Dandy Suit and Action Routes', in Haining, Peter, *The Doctor Who File*, p118.)

return to overt humour, both in scripting and performance.

A Second Blitzkrieg: The Hitchhiking Years (1978-79)

With the departure of Producer Philip Hinchcliffe and Script Editor Robert Holmes, Tom Baker was unleashed, ad-libbing to an almost unpardonable extent; yet Baker's character was also written in a more light-hearted fashion, allowing the Doctor in the late '70s to become the same kind of distracted Mr Magoo turned volatile, tetchy aristocrat that William Hartnell portrayed so distinctively in and around the time of *The Romans*.

With humour to be the driving force, it is perhaps not altogether surprising that a young Douglas Adams was at this time drawn to **Doctor Who** and gave the programme its second comedic trilogy. Adams wrote *The Pirate Planet* (1978) and *Shada* (unaired, 1980), both of which were intellectual SF comedies in the **Hitchhiker's** vein, while as Script Editor for season 17 he reworked David Fisher's Bulldog Drummond spoof 'The Gamble with Time' as *City of Death* (1979). Adams' involvement was in this sense much like Donald Cotton's had been[39]. However, whereas Cotton and Adams themselves both followed the comedic template laid down by *The Romans* – funny, offset by serious – there clung to Adams a tenacious misconception that his humour was all about jokiness.

Then came new Producer John Nathan-Turner.

---

[39] For a more detailed comparison of Adams and Cotton, and of their respective contributions to **Who**, see Edwards, Jacob, 'In the Shadow of Slartibartfast: Donald Cotton and **Doctor Who**'s Other Comedic Trilogy'.

Exaggeratingly Po-Faced (1980-84)

Nathan-Turner swept in as **Doctor Who**'s new broom, and out went the comedy. Season 18's opening story *The Leisure Hive* (1980), for example, was to have been a Mafia spoof, yet for all that David Fisher's novelisation (1982) reads like an Adams pastiche[40], the story as broadcast is near enough entirely without laughs; the closest it came to tickling the funny bone was half a year later when the Foamasi costume was recycled for that of the G'Gugvuntt leader in the BBC television adaptation of **The Hitchhiker's Guide to the Galaxy**[41]. In the meantime, Tom Baker's swansong season bled into three years of utter sincerity from Peter Davison[42]. This, again, was a backlash against the preceding humour, and it couldn't last. When the fifth Doctor met his demise on Androzani, the ebb in comedy gave way to perhaps its most controversial flow: Colin Baker.

A Throwback to Gallows Humour (1985-86)

The sixth Doctor had a sense of humour that certain swathes of the viewership could not bring themselves to countenance. In

---

[40] A similar, pseudo-Adamsesque approach was taken by Eric Saward in scripting and then novelising the sixth Doctor radio play *Slipback* (1985/1986).

[41] 'The Leisure Hive'. *Whotopia.*

[42] Davison's characterisation of the Doctor is perhaps the most nuanced of all, incorporating a subtle lightening of the mood where needed. In terms of scripted humour, however, the only hint of relief comes in *The Visitation* (1982), where writer Eric Saward reused the overblown character Richard Mace from some of his non-**Who** radio plays, and in *Black Orchid* (1982) when the Doctor invites some early 20th-century policemen into the TARDIS, which, as comedic material goes, is hardly side-splitting.

Vengeance on Varos (1985), he addresses what seems a callously flippant remark to the bubbling acid bath where two guards – having just tried to execute him – have met their grisly end: 'Forgive me if I don't join you.'[43] In *The Two Doctors* (1985), he attacks and kills the murderously cannibalistic (more or less) Shockeye – an extreme act for the Doctor, even in self-defence – and then quips, 'Your just desserts.'[44] This, some people felt, lacked empathy; it just wasn't how the Doctor should behave. In the *Varos* audio commentary, Colin Baker offered the following defence: 'The Doctor is appalled. However, he deals with it. He's an alien, so he doesn't do what you or I would do. He makes a joke.'

This is a perfectly valid point, and is consistent with the way Baker acted the part. Curiously, though, the sixth Doctor's ostensibly callous gallows humour is exactly what Derek Francis brought to Nero in *The Romans*. Granted, Nero is the villain, not the hero; and yet, the fifth Doctor also got away with a rather grim quip in part 2 of *The Awakening* (1984), where the prospect of the May Queen being burnt alive elicits from him the (tellingly self-aware) observation: 'The toast of Little Hodcombe.' Acting strengths aside, the difference, it would appear, is that a groundswell of (misplaced) antipathy towards Baker's Doctor led to an almost wilful misconstruing of the not-comedy. Whatever precedent *The Romans* may have set, by Baker's time it was being disregarded.

The Untethered Future (Post-Colin Baker)

This, then, might be a good spot to break off our charting of *The*

---

43 *Vengeance on Varos* episode 2.
44 *The Two Doctors* episode 3.

Romans' comedic legacy. Sylvester McCoy certainly had his moments as the seventh Doctor (much in the Patrick Troughton mould), while, post-cancellation, Paul McGann's and Richard E Grant's portrayals of the eighth and one-time ninth Doctors were brief beyond measure.

Twenty-first century **Who** has proven a whole new kettle of fish.

The revamped series brought incidental humour aplenty, plus more extensive deployment in, for example, the farce of *Partners in Crime* and the outright comedy of *The Unicorn and the Wasp* (2008). Starting with Christopher Eccleston's obliviousness to the London Eye and belated, beaming call of 'Fantastic!' in *Rose* (2005), **Doctor Who** in the new millennium has proven itself consistently and pleasingly funny; so much so, that the programme's two eras seem in this respect quite distinct. New Series **Who** did eventually return to Roman times, yet when writer James Moran was given his brief for *The Fires of Pompeii* he was unaware of *The Romans*[45]. He looked it up, and there's a lovely bit of metatextual drollery when Donna tests the TARDIS's translation circuits and her Latin comes out 'Celtic', but still there is little sense of a torch passed between the two serials; just a freestyling shout-out that surfaces briefly amidst the tenth Doctor's ebullient nattering: 'Before you ask, that fire had nothing to do with me ... Well, a little bit.'

Though a nice reminder of where the comedy began, *The Fires of Pompeii* is evidence that **Doctor Who** has moved on, outgrowing any connection to *The Romans*. **Who** in the 21st century will

---

[45] 'What Has *The Romans* Ever Done For Us?' *The Romans* DVD extra.

happily give a nod to its past – it will even call upon that past to help legitimise itself – but the latter-day programme is very much its own creature. If any closure is required for this move to independence, it comes by way of *Twice Upon a Time* (2017), when the dazed First World War Captain approaches the TARDIS and inquires of the first and twelfth Doctors, 'I don't suppose either of you is a doctor?'. Both Doctors look at each other but it is Peter Capaldi's modern incarnation not David Bradley's forerunner who retorts, 'You trying to be funny?'

CHAPTER 4: WHAT ELSE WAS NEW IN *THE ROMANS*?

The Romans' place in history is assured. It was **Doctor Who**'s first concerted foray into humour, and will always be remembered as such. Comedy aside, though, *The Romans* introduced several other concepts – two from a production standpoint, one from scripting – that would become mainstays of the programme; notions we now take for granted but without which transformations our memories of **Doctor Who** would be very different.

Even once the laughter of *The Romans* died down and normal service was resumed, **Doctor Who** found itself irrevocably changed.

The Four-Part Story Structure

It may at first appear odd to suggest that *The Romans* introduced the four-part structure to **Doctor Who**. After all, the programme's very first story – *An Unearthly Child* (1963) – was four episodes long, as was season 1's *The Aztecs* (1964)[46]. Yet, *An Unearthly Child* was more accurately the pilot episode welded onto a three-part story; and *The Aztecs*, while **happening** to be a four-parter, seems something of an outlier, or even just the inevitable oddity in what already was a seasonal mixed-bag.

From *The Romans* onwards, there comes a distinct sense that stories were being commissioned at four parts for reasons of

---

[46] *Planet of Giants* (1964) had also been scripted at four, but for pacing reasons was compacted to three.

narrative value, not production[47]. This isn't to say that the four-part structure was dramatically perfect (third episode let-down would become a perennial problem); nor that production costs weren't still a limiting factor: though unrelated by plot, *The Rescue* and *The Romans* were blocked together, forming a similar 2-part, 4-part combo as later seen in *The Ark in Space* (1975) and *The Sontaran Experiment* (1975) and then *The Trial of a Time Lord* (1986) parts 9-12 and parts 13-14. But *The Romans*, written by incoming Script Editor Dennis Spooner, was **very deliberately** a four-parter, and for some time afterwards four-parters became the dominant strain.

While David Whitaker was Script Editor, only 2 of 10 stories were four-parters. During Spooner's tenure, this figure climbed to 3 of 6, and of the next 21 stories – from *The Time Meddler* to *The Tomb of the Cybermen* – 16 were four-parters. All told, the majority of **Doctor Who** serials in the 20th century – 96 of 158 – took the four-part structure. One can argue to what extent this particular wheel was reinvented over the years, but we should give at least some credit where first due: in terms of intent, it started with *The Romans*.

---

[47] The difference is summed up by 1970s director and former production assistant Michael Briant in the audio commentary to *The Power of the Daleks* episode 6:

> 'Four-part **Who**s were always better than six-part **Who**s. Four parts it was possible to have, more or less, a beginning, middle and end; and a six-parter you always had at least one episode, if not two, which was just padding; and the only reason six-parters were made was it was cheaper... It cost exactly the same money to make four episodes in terms of scenery as it did for six.'

Famous Guest Stars

Viewers raised on 21st-century **Who** will quite possibly take guest stars for granted. It wasn't always so.

Doctor Who from the outset was scripted heavily around its four leads, giving them by far the lion's share of screen time and dialogue. *The Romans* for the first time afforded equal footing to a non-regular: Derek Francis as Nero[48].

Francis was a good friend of Alvin Rakoff (Jacqueline Hill's husband), and had been promised a role in the show since the start[49]. The effect of his casting was twofold. Firstly, Spooner recalls altering the script:

> 'Derek Francis wasn't my first choice for the part. [...] He was offered the role of Nero because he was a friend of the family, and I couldn't resist writing in the sequence when he tried to seduce Barbara. "Best friends always try to seduce the wife," I told him...'[50]

In other words, it seems that Nero's woo-hooing of Barbara – a plot point that underpins the farce of 'Conspiracy' – may only have come about by way of a concatenation of off-screen relationships!

---

[48] George Coulouris was a bigger name, but this is hardly reflected in the prominence given to his character (Arbitan in *The Keys of Marinus*). Of the guest performers prior to *The Romans*, not even Mark Eden, for all his aplomb playing the titular role in *Marco Polo*, was entrusted with as much responsibility as was Francis.
[49] Pixley, Andrew, *Doctor Who: The Complete History* volume 4, p95.
[50] Quoted in Peel, John, 'Character Profiles', *Doctor Who: An Adventure in Space and Time* #M: *The Romans*, p8.

Secondly, **Doctor Who** gained its first bona fide guest star. Derek Francis came to prominence on stage in the late 1950s, appearing in numerous Shakespearian plays (most notably as the titular role in *Cymbeline*, 1957) at the Old Vic. He had several minor film parts in the early 1960s before gaining recognition (third billing) as Jack Carter in *The Hi-Jackers* (1963). In the years leading up to *The Romans*, Francis was most famous for playing dramatic small-screen parts: Gaston Rondeur in the 7-episode POW drama *The Long Way Home* (1960); Joey Walker in the BBC's 13-episode drama/thriller *The Six Proud Walkers* (1962); Tillio Grunditz in 6-episode thriller *The Midnight Men* (1964); as well as significant roles in four instalments each of **ITV Television Playhouse** (1959-63) and **BBC Sunday-Night Play** (1960-63). Francis was a name actor, and in Spooner's scripting of Nero there lay material genuinely worthy of a guest star. Francis not only did the part justice but also paved the way for **Doctor Who** to feature substantial contributions by non-regulars.

What followed – slowly at first – was a shift towards stronger guest roles and more notable guest actors: Max Adrian in *The Myth Makers*, for instance, and Michael Gough in *The Celestial Toymaker* (1966). William Hartnell is said to have resented the attention given to Adrian[51]; but given that he'd had no such difficulty with Francis, his own illness and insecurities seem a more likely cause of his discontent on set. Either way, Producer John Wiles (Verity Lambert's successor) was unimpressed[52], and there remains food

---

[51] Pixley, Andrew, **Doctor Who**: *The Complete History* volume 6, p81.
[52] Wood and Miles, *About Time* #1, p208.

for thought in Michael Gough's having been cast in the same serial wherein Wiles had intended to replace Hartnell altogether[53]. This wouldn't have been regeneration as we now know it, but rather the straight substitution of one actor for another playing the same character. Although this didn't occur, the powers that be were coming to appreciate the potential of casting high-profile non-regulars: for all that Hartnell was **Doctor Who**'s face, if one stretched one's imagination in the right direction then it was possible to conceive of not only him but also the Doctor himself as being mere 'guests' within the show's unfolding narrative.

Again, this started with *The Romans*.

The twinkling of guest stars continued after Hartnell's departure – Marius Goring in *The Evil of the Daleks* (1967), for example, Ingrid Pitt in *The Time Monster* (1972) and Julian Glover in *City of Death* – and the newfound respectability of **Doctor Who** began also to show itself further down the cast list. In Tom Baker's era it became almost de rigueur for actors, in appeasement of their children, to take a role (any role) in **Who**. This, no doubt, was for the betterment of the programme... until suddenly it wasn't.

The first instance of celebrity casting[54] came when Douglas Adams persuaded John Cleese and Eleanor Bron to play art critics in *City of Death*. The problem here lay not in the quality of performance, but

---

[53] Wood and Miles, *About Time* #1, p260.
[54] Or as it is sometimes referred to, stunt casting. Whereas modern-day **Who** leans towards genuine guest stars – notable actors cast for what they bring to the finished product – stunt casting seeks instead those actors whose involvement will generate the most publicity.

in the fact that the roles were superfluous; gratuitous cameos that contributed not one iota to the story (and hence no doubt came as a disappointment to anyone who'd tuned in specially). It wasn't even Adams' job to make casting decisions. Presumably it just struck him as a good idea at the time.

Unfortunately, this one-off piece of opportunism from Adams turned to mandated policy under 1980s Producer John Nathan-Turner. To be sure, there were mitigating circumstances – budgetary cutbacks that drove Nathan-Turner ever more to seek publicity over substance – but there's no denying he went out of his way to put big names in the *Radio Times*, squeezing stars into scripts that had no real place for them[55], and hiring actors whose performances weren't controlled[56], or who were just fundamentally unsuited[57]. Nathan-Turner had several such moments of madness, perhaps the most outrageous being when he offered Laurence Olivier (who had actually agreed in principle to a small guest role in **Doctor Who**) the part of a swamp-drenched, snarling mutant[58].

Had Olivier not politely declined to facilitate this nadir, it too would have been – albeit at some merciful distance removed – the end product of a shift that began with *The Romans*.

---

[55] Stubby Kaye in *Delta and the Bannermen* (1987); Dolores Gray in *Silver Nemesis* (1988).

[56] Alexei Sayle in *Revelation of the Daleks* (1985); Richard Briers in *Paradise Towers* (1987).

[57] Hale and Pace in *Survival* (1989). To be fair, Beryl Reid (*Earthshock*, 1982) isn't as off-target as most people suppose; and Nicholas Parsons (*The Curse of Fenric*, 1989) is more or less a win.

[58] Albeit one not entirely without dramatic potential. In *Revelation of the Daleks* (1985). Wood, Tat, *About Time #6*, p105.

Making History

Without doubt, *The Romans* changed **Doctor Who** in another key way: it marks the programme's fundamental about-face vis-à-vis the past.

In his writers' guide of July 1963, inaugural Script Editor David Whitaker had warned prospective **Who** contributors:

> 'It is also emphasised that the four characters cannot make history. Advice must not be proffered to Nelson on his battle tactics when approaching the Nile nor must bon mots be put into the mouth of Oscar Wilde.'[59]

In light of what **Doctor Who** would become, this seems rather a quaint notion. But Whitaker couldn't have known that the Doctor, through dramatic necessity and increasingly offhandedly across 50-plus years of television, would eventually play some part in just about every key moment of Earth's history. The rule for the first (and as far as anyone knew, only) season of **Doctor Who** was that history was sacrosanct. It was there to be explored, caught up in and disentangled from. Established events were not to be subverted.

That didn't mean the characters couldn't try. Barbara in *The Aztecs* seizes upon what she perceives as a golden opportunity to advance civilisation: having been mistaken for the goddess Yetaxa, she can use her divine authority to promote rationalism, thereby dissuading the Aztecs from human sacrifice and instead ushering them into a golden era. Barbara may have gone a bit time-and-space crazy – her

---

[59] Quoted in Chapman, James, *Inside the TARDIS*, p20.

plan, if successful, would mangle history – and yet she is quite earnest.

The Doctor is dead set against the elevation of the Aztecs, and indeed keeps to his staunchly non-interventionist stance throughout most of Hartnell's tenure. He won't, for instance, let Steven save Anne Chaplet from the eponymous *Massacre of St Bartholomew's Eve* (1966)[60], his proscription thereafter resulting in the same sort of friction between him and Steven as would present between the 10th Doctor and Donna in *The Fires of Pompeii*. This despite that, in the very next story – *The Ark* (1966) – the Doctor, Steven and Dodo proceed very conspicuously (if unintentionally) to derail the course of Human and Monoid history in the far future.

By the time the 10th Doctor came not to intervene at Pompeii, the programme's seeming inconsistencies were being rationalised as the result of 'fixed' and 'flux' moments in history; in other words, those events that are too ingrained to be changed, and those that are superficial enough for the universe to shrug off. Back in the first Doctor's day, this distinction was still far from having been made. Instead, we are faced with someone who **isn't really sure** and who, for all his authoritarian bluster, is half convinced he should be walking about on eggshells.

To shift analogies, the Doctor at this time is a compulsive and exuberant lepidopterist... who lives in fear of the butterfly effect. Not able to leave well enough alone, he tries extra hard not to step on anything.

---

[60] Cf. *Doctor Who* (1996) in which Paul McGann's Doctor alludes to a calamity of similar magnitude and warns Lee to steer clear of San Francisco.

Until the Great Fire of Rome.

The Romans, as we know, is a comedy, and the Doctor ambles through its historical setting in a mostly affable and carefree manner. He is particularly indulgent of Vicki – a surrogate for his recently departed granddaughter – and yet reacts strongly when she confesses to having switched poisoned drinks on Nero[61]. The Doctor's demeanour shifts in an instant. ('And I told you not to interfere with history! Come along. Quickly; quickly, child!') *The Romans* may be playing for laughs; 'Conspiracy' may be known for its farce; but even so, the ramifications of Vicki's actions bring us heavily back down to earth. Nero poisoned in 64 CE? That's serious business[62]. History **would** be changed.

Which brings us to a watershed moment. It comes in 'Inferno' at almost exactly the same point in that episode. The Doctor and Vicki are gazing over one of the seven hills to where Rome is burning, and Vicki calls the Doctor out[63]:

VICKI

Honestly, Doctor! And after that long talk you gave me about not meddling with history. You ought to be ashamed of yourself.

DOCTOR

It's got nothing to do with **me**.

---

[61] 'Conspiracy'.
[62] A vital and oft-neglected component of successful comedy.
[63] 'Inferno'.

VICKI

You burnt his drawings!

DOCTOR

Oh, yes. An accident!

VICKI

Well, maybe it was, but if you hadn't –

DOCTOR

He would have – he could have – You can't possibly accuse me of that!

VICKI

All right. You have it your way, I'll have it mine.

DOCTOR

Now look here, young lady, let's settle this! Insinuating that all this is **my** fault... Hmm? Hmm. My fault... Hm-hmm. Ha-ha! Hoo-hoo! Hmmmm!

The Doctor starts out impartial; content, in fact, to be witness to one of history's great events. When Vicki accuses him, he is at first affronted, then laughs off her suggestion. When she persists, he becomes flustered, backpedalling from what would be an uncomfortable truth. He puts his foot down once more to deny it... but then realisation dawns: he **was** responsible; for all his talk against the idea, he **did** bring about the Great Fire of Rome.

It's not an epiphany that will lead at once to wholescale historical revisionism – for the immediate future that is the purview of the

Monk, not the Doctor – and yet this is it; this is when the Doctor first truly opens his eyes to a universe of possibility.

Changing history? Suddenly the notion tickles his fancy.

CHAPTER 5: WHAT IS HISTORY?

Time travel is one of the fundamental aspects of **Doctor Who**, and on several occasions over the years the programme has taken a position on changing history. Can it be done? Should it be done? **Must** it be done?

All those thwarted invasions of Earth – should we see those as aliens trying to alter the course of a universe in which our little blue-green planet is destined to thrive? Or is it the Doctor who is messing the timelines about, intervening with hindsight as a naturalist would if given the power to go back and save the last dodo?

Are there really fixed points that can't be changed (*The Fires of Pompeii*)? Is it truly impossible to delve back into events you've already played a part in (*Time-Flight*, 1982)? Is meeting an earlier version of yourself genuinely catastrophic (*Mawdryn Undead*, 1983) or just a terrible power drain (*The Three Doctors*, 1972-73)? Is nothing more binding than a time paradox (*The Angels Take Manhattan*, 2012)?[64]

The prosaic answer to all these questions is: don't think about it too much; drama dictates and the plot has its own demands.

But if we **are** going to think about it then the real question must be: what is history?

The answer most people gravitate towards (without necessarily

---

[64] Or is fatalism itself the limiting factor? If Amy and Rory were of a mind to, could they not pay for their tombstone, walk clear of New York and rendezvous with the Doctor elsewhere?

even putting it into words) is that history is what happened in the past. To anyone who doesn't flit about the timelines, this would make perfect sense; but to aficionados of time travel it immediately raises the issue of perspective.

Prior to travelling with the Doctor, Vicki would naturally consider the Great Fire of Rome to be something that has already taken place. It is history. And yet, given that she will one day step into a time machine, it is also an event from her future. While she is in Rome, events unfold in the present tense. So, why **not** intervene? In this sense, history would be like a stunt car on the loop-the-loop: history as Vicki knows it (the general past) burns along the track to the point where she enters the TARDIS; the time she spends with the Doctor is then all one big looping present tense; and finally, once she is no longer a time traveller, history resumes and the future proceeds to play out, its track angled ever so slightly differently from the vector of approach[65].

History in this interpretation **is** what happened in the past... but only after it has become the personal past of everyone who might loop through it from elsewhen in timelines untethered. The Doctor is right, therefore, in claiming that he didn't change history. Nero **would** have come up with the idea anyway; did, in fact. The Doctor only became part of events once his personal past looped beyond

---

[65] Indeed, Vicki's life beyond time travel sees her take up residence in what, from perspective of her birth year, would be very ancient history, running off with Troilus at the end of the Trojan War and (presumably) playing some part in those events that inspired Virgil's *Aeneid*.

the events of 64 CE[66].

In this sense, Vicki also is correct: the history books – assuming the next one she picks up hasn't rewritten itself to reflect the change – omitted the Doctor's contribution and therefore got it wrong. History books are in fact doing this all the time, and historians spend much of their analytical powers trying to reconstruct actual events in the face of an incomplete or actively duplicitous written record. Nero, by current estimation, was not even in Rome when the fire started[67]. But even that fact is just our best interpretation of the evidence; by the conceit of time travel, Vicki has incontrovertible proof to the contrary. Recorded history is wrong.

Such, ultimately, is the rub; and just as Isaac Asimov in *The Naked Sun* (1957) revised his First Law of Robotics to include the implicit caveat: 'A robot may do nothing that, **to its knowledge**, will harm a human being; nor, through inaction, **knowingly** allow a human being to come to harm[68]'; so too does the Doctor's early diktat require amendment. If history is only what we think we know to have happened, based more often on consensus than physical

---

[66] This point is complicated by our not knowing where Gallifrey's past stands in relation to Earth's, and hence to the writing of Earth's history. Established canon notwithstanding, the Time Lords' mastery of causality would most plausibly situate them at the beginning of the universe; hence, any change they were to bring about would be an alteration of an observed – but not yet ratified – future. Or something like that.

[67] Griffin, Miriam T, *Nero: The End of a Dynasty*, p132. Although first published in 1984, as of 2019 Griffin's text remains unchallenged on this point.

[68] Asimov, Isaac, *The Naked Sun*, pp148-49.

evidence, then any tut-tutting or pronouncement of 'Thou shalt not meddle with history' is essentially meaningless. If Vicki were to succeed in poisoning Nero, chances are she wouldn't change history. Not really. The record would reassert itself: the poison would prove ineffective; or Nero would die and be replaced by an impersonator; or…

Or just possibly not. Another alternative is that the loop-the-loop would burn itself up and send causality calling; a fiery paradox sweeping through time, reducing Vicki to ashes.

Which would it be? The Doctor, we may suspect, doesn't actually know. At this point in his temporal wanderings he is not so much an expert as a gentleman dilettante. He blunders in with ingrained self-assurance, then ignorance leaves him all of a dither.

Don't mess with history, the Doctor insists… but only when he happens to think about it. When it comes to satisfying his own whims – impersonating the recently deceased Maximus Pettulian, for example, so as to meet with Nero – he evinces not a care in the world. The double standard is even more evident in Cotton's novelisation, where the Doctor not only plays an inadvertent role in making history – knocking the arms off a statue of Venus; setting fire to Nero's plans[69] – but also takes it upon himself to buttonhole the emperor and put forward proposals for civil reform[70]. Cotton, of course, writes in jest; and yet still he makes a valid point: in terms of historical consequence, there is no practical difference between active interference and unintended repercussion. For all that the

---

[69] Cotton, *The Romans*, pp112-13, 63.
[70] Cotton, *The Romans* p84.

Doctor might scold Vicki, he himself is every bit as culpable.

The differences between Cotton's novelisation and *The Romans* as broadcast are particularly interesting vis-à-vis time travel. Ian, for instance, spends the entire book under the misapprehension that any action he performs in his own general past (the 60s CE) must ipso facto take place before actions from a relative general future (the **19**60s), regardless of his personal experiences. Hence he writes of the Doctor:

> 'Once more I can only regret the impulse of misguided curiosity which first led me to become entangled in his eccentric, torturous, and altogether incomprehensible affairs. Or rather, which **will** one day lead me to become so entangled; for, since we have been travelling **backwards** in time, I suppose I haven't met him yet. How very difficult this all is! Well, in that case, when I **do** meet him for the first time, I shall do my utmost not to recognise him, and see how he likes that!'[71]

Cotton is taking the mickey; but again, a serious point lies beneath the humour: how much of what we read in the novelisations or see on TV is true history even within the fictional universe of **Doctor Who**? Are we to take *The Romans* at face value? Or is it just a tall tale; a regular historical adventure hammed up in the telling?

In other words, do the events of **Doctor Who** take place within some kind of miniscope[72], unfolding exactly as we see them? Or is **Doctor Who** more like a biopic, filtering a true story through the

---

[71] Cotton, *The Romans* p13.
[72] As featured in *Carnival of Monsters* (1973).

creative lens of an unreliable filmmaker?

The Romans does not purport to ask such questions, let alone answer them; and yet, an entire theoretical discipline has sprung to prominence allowing us to conscript it to this very purpose: postmodernism.

Intrinsic to the more laudable branches of Postmodernism is a resolve to balance out the historical record; to interpret events from minority or otherwise un- or under-represented viewpoints[73]. In its extreme manifestations, however, postmodernism goes well beyond this. Instead of reconstructing lost perspectives, it retrofits modern ideas onto those it purports to represent; even onto those who overtly disavow such ideas. It doesn't interpret the written record and physical evidence so much as – often most belligerently – ignore or repudiate it[74]. From high-minded ideals, then, postmodernism can all too easily degenerate to the point where it makes no distinction between history and fiction. In the postmodernist world there is no fact, only interpretation. Moreover, there is no mechanism, other than individual belief, for deciding between conflicting assertions. All theories are equally valid[75].

---

[73] Duignan, Brian, 'Postmodernism'.

[74] For an accessible academic discussion of such absurdities – including a chapter on the downfall of the Aztecs – the reader is directed to Windschuttle, Keith, *The Killing of History*.

[75] Except, perhaps, where there is hard evidence to support them. Postmodernism tends to view evidence as intrinsically untrustworthy. Interpretations of history sans empirical support

Curiously enough, this bewildering concept of notional veracity – the many malleable truths of history – is not so far removed from cutting-edge scientific theory. In science fiction (particularly time travel stories), paradoxes such as Vicki's poisoning of Nero – had it happened – used to be explained by the branching of events into parallel universes. Every choice, every action taken or decided against, no matter how inconsequential, led to the creation of a new universe; realms where each could-have-been scenario turned out to have received an upgrade to was-in-fact[76].

Fiction nowadays has moved on, and science with it, affording less room for choice. By modern conjecture, parallel universes aren't created; they exist already, layered infinitely to constitute what we refer to as the multiverse. Here, every eventuality plays out, regardless of who's making what decisions. So long as the laws of physics don't prohibit it, it happens[77]. The Boy Who Cried Wolf?

---

seem generally to outweigh the perfidious machinations of recorded fact (so-called).

[76] Sadly, the parallel worlds thus generated bore no practical value to the decision maker, save for their theoretical value as proof against grandfathers rendered prematurely dead.

[77] For more on this and other rather fantabulous-sounding notions, see Deutsch, David, *The Beginning of Infinity*, p452. Where the multiverse potentially proves of more practical use than parallel universes is in the pre-existence of all outcomes. This key difference provides the underpinning for quantum computing, where, instead of solving equations by brute force trial and error over untold zillions of attempts, the computer isolates that one improbable iteration of the multiverse in which it stumbled upon the correct answer at first try (Gribbin, John, *Computing with Quantum Cats*, p207).

Historical fact. *Ferris Bueller's Day Off* (1986)? True story. So, of course, somewhere in the multiverse a girl named Vicki **did** arrive in Rome with an old man called the Doctor (but posing as a Corinthian lyre player by name of Maximus Pettulian). Somewhere, she **did** meet the official court poisoner, Locusta. Somewhere, she switched goblets and came within a whisker of killing the Emperor Nero.

While somewhere else — not necessarily a different iteration of the multiverse, but probably — Dennis Spooner recorded that same story in the form of a **Doctor Who** script, which Christopher Barry then directed for broadcast by the BBC.

Somewhere else again, this not only happened but also was exactly what Sydney Newman intended when he mandated that **Doctor Who**'s historical stories be factually accurate and fit for educational purposes...

History, it turns out, is a funny thing.

CHAPTER 6: WHERE DID *THE ROMANS* COME FROM?

If one were to conduct a survey asking writers for a shortlist of historical periods in which to set a story, chances are that Ancient Rome would feature prominently. People **know** Rome, or at least think they do; and as Wood and Miles point out, this would certainly have been the case for the viewership of England, 1965, who until recently had been force-fed Latin – and therefore Roman history – at school[78].

If tasked with narrowing down the setting, our surveyed writers would likely default to the early Roman Empire. This period is laid open to us particularly by the ancient writer Suetonius in *The Twelve Caesars* (121 CE), a dozen muckraking biographies starting with Julius Caesar and proceeding through the first 11 emperors of Rome[79]. The fledgling days of the Empire were further popularised by Robert Graves' historical novels *I, Claudius* (1934) and *Claudius the God* (1935), which prior to *The Romans* were sufficiently well received as to have been reprinted multiple times. In 1963, the epic American feature film *Cleopatra* swept the box office, thereby pushing Rome still further into the public consciousness[80].

Rome, in other words, was ripe for the picking; it is little wonder that departing Script Editor David Whitaker proposed it for one of

---

[78] Wood and Miles, *About Time* #1, p127.
[79] Augustus, Tiberius, Caligula, Claudius, Nero, Galba, Otho, Vitellius, Vespasian, Titus and Domitian.
[80] Followed less successfully by *The Fall of the Roman Empire* in 1964.

Doctor Who's historical adventures[81].

Whitaker, however, by this time in the show's production, was disillusioned at having to feature real historical personages[82]. This is perhaps unsurprising. **Doctor Who**'s educational remit, we might imagine, would quickly have turned into something of a millstone around the writers' necks. (There is, after all, something quite artificial in the need to squeeze action drama into known events.) Dennis Spooner, judging from his then-recent, not especially accurate depiction of the French Revolution's Reign of Terror, seems also to have chafed at history's constraints.

How, then, do we explain *The Romans*, which features a host of known historical figures, principal among them the emperor himself? The rationale is more easily discernible if we look beyond Dennis Spooner's historical comedy to that of Donald Cotton.

Donald Cotton played loose to make merry with history, spurning any attempt at a genuine historical setting and offering up instead an amalgam of historical titbits and non-specific exemplars. Although nominally based on the Gunfight at the OK Corral, *The Gunfighters* is more true to the Western genre in toto than to documented history. *The Myth Makers*, likewise, is more a play on historical epics in general than a true account of the Trojan War (even as romanticised by Homer). Both serials pay lip service to history but derive their humour from caricaturing nebulous modern perceptions of the periods in question.

---

[81] Third in line after stories set respectively in the aftermath of the Spanish Armada and during the American Civil War (Wood and Miles, *About Time* #1 p129).
[82] Wood and Miles, *About Time* #1 p129.

The Romans anticipates this approach to historical comedy. The Great Fire notwithstanding, it could have been set at almost any point in the history of the Roman Empire and need not have referenced Nero explicitly. It is a story of tropes – slavery, lust, decadence, intrigue – and though the figures of history are there to be recognised, should one be of a mind to, they are as much exaggerated stage characters as real people. History, in this sense, no longer falls within the purview of education. The details, where present, are unimportant, and *The Romans* does not seek to teach us about Nero himself or indeed anything much at all. Comedy is the dish of the day; it is also the means by which the poison is delivered. On Dennis Spooner's watch, history loses its sacrosanctity and becomes just another (easily recognisable) backdrop against which to tell a story.

It was David Whittaker's idea to set a **Doctor Who** historical in Ancient Rome, and Verity Lambert's to make this a comedy[83]. The exact nature of the humour was down to Dennis Spooner, who had two inspirations close at hand. The most recent of these was *Carry On Cleo*[84], a spoof of the aforementioned *Cleopatra*. Although *Carry on Cleo* was released only late in 1964, Spooner had recently co-written the mini-series *Ring-a-Ding-Ding* (1964) with one of its stars, Jim Dale:

> 'There had been a classic Nero in *Quo Vadis* [1951], so I suppose we were sending up *Quo Vadis*. There was this **Carry On**... film in production – *Carry on Cleo* – and at that time I virtually lived next door to Jim Dale who was in the

---

[83] *The Complete History*, Volume 4, pp90-91.
[84] Wood and Miles, *About Time* #1 p127. '

film. When I was writing *The Romans*, I went down to Pinewood to watch him in the filming; so my story was heavily influenced by *Carry on Cleo*. We had the same researcher, and the **Carry On**... films were never very serious with their research ... Gertan Klauber was in both; that wasn't a coincidence – that's where it all came from!'[85]

However, while *Carry On Cleo* may have informed the more infantile scenes in *The Romans* episode 3, Spooner himself more broadly credited *A Funny Thing Happened on the Way to the Forum* (the musical comedy). *A Funny Thing* was very popular, notching up 964 performances on Broadway and then 762 in London[86]. This not only accustomed the public still further to Ancient Rome, but also forged an overt link between Rome and comedy.

Where *Carry On Cleo* is quintessentially a lowbrow ménage à trois of puns, pratfalls and puerility, *A Funny Thing* features an underlying satire of the social class system, and is driven by a relentless farce of chance meetings and mistaken identities. This isn't to say that its humour is anything more than comparatively highbrow; only that the difference between *Carry On Cleo* and *A Funny Thing*[87] is roughly akin to that between the runaround of 'Conspiracy' and *The Romans*' more measured merriment

---

[85] Spooner, quoted in Tulloch, John, and Manuel Alvarado, *Doctor Who: The Unfolding Text*, pp156-57.
[86] The London production starred future Doctor Jon Pertwee as Marcus Lycus.
[87] The stage version, at any rate; a much rewritten film interpretation (1966) threw out Burt Shevelove's and Larry Gelbart's original libretto, seemingly with a view to scrumping some of **Carry On**'s stock trade in fruitiness.

elsewhere.

A Funny Thing is not tied to a precise date in history. It has, in effect, a stock setting; a period in time sufficient for us to picture it but no more distinct than the notional bar in any joke beginning: 'A man walks into a bar...' As *The Romans* paid tribute to *A Funny Thing*, so too was *A Funny Thing* an homage to the ancient Roman playwright Plautus (251-183 BCE), a noted comedian who reworked Greek productions and was known for both his wordplay and his use of archetypal characters such as the sly and clever slave (Tavius), the flatterer (Tigilinus) and the lecherous old man (Nero)[88].

The Romans, then, is historical comedy based on historical comedy. It is – albeit by several degrees removed and with the serial numbers filed off – the genuine article.

It is history repeating.

---

[88] Hornblower, Simon and Antony Spawforth, eds, *The Oxford Classical Dictionary*, p1195.

CHAPTER 7: HOW HISTORICALLY ACCURATE IS *THE ROMANS*?

Given that **Doctor Who**'s historical adventures were supposed to be educational, this looks at first a pertinent question. With the Doctor's fictional injunction against changing history, it would appear especially so.

We have seen, however, that history is hard to pin down, and that the production staff were by the time of *The Romans* no longer committed to vouchsafing its depiction[89].

It would seem churlish, then, to pick apart *The Romans* in search of such trifling details as misaligned plinths and tarnished imperial brass. Suffice here to say that the serial's overall effect is positive; for the purposes of one-off drama the quiddities were more than adequate.

Having said that, there **are** a few misrepresentations that can't, in all good collective conscience, be left unchecked:

- Derek Francis was 41 years old when he played Nero, whereas the emperor – who died at age 30 – was only 26 when the Great Fire broke out. Nero was fair-haired, and by what we can tell from statuary busts (admittedly not the

---

[89] The justification for this change of policy would be that stimulating **interest** in historical events was more important than sticking dully to the facts. Sydney Newman had always thought that exposure to history would inspire children to then seek it out in textbooks ('The Slave Traders' audio commentary). Now, the inspiration would come less from any intrinsic appeal and more from history's association with **Doctor Who**.

most reliable of sources) looked not unlike John Belushi in *The Blues Brothers* (1980), except with the sideburns continuing on to form a kind of bonnet strap beneath the chin. Facially, Derek Francis isn't a million miles away, and it was a nice touch by the hair stylist to give him a sawblade fringe. Nevertheless, it seems clear that Francis was cast for the performance he could give, not for any great physical resemblance to the emperor. If we were to draw our mental picture of Nero solely from *The Romans*[90], history would shift uneasily in its grave.

- The big reveal of Tavius' Christianity comes by way of the cross he wears on a necklace hidden beneath his tunic. This is a convenient telltale but also a glaring anachronism. The cross – particularly one whose shape wasn't obfuscated – wouldn't be embraced as a Christian symbol until several hundred years later[91]; wearing one during Nero's time would have been macabre at best, and quite likely very dangerous[92].

---

[90] Either the televised serial or Donald Cotton's novelisation, the cover art of which (by Tony Masero) references but materially distorts Peter Ustinov's itself-not-unreasonable approximation of Nero in *Quo Vadis*.

[91] Wilson, Ralph F, 'Early Christian Symbols of the Ancient Church from the Catacombs'.

[92] Christianity, being monotheistic, precluded the worship of other gods. The Roman religion was pantheistic but nevertheless demanded at least ceremonial first loyalty to the Emperor. Even if there is some debate as to whether the imperial cult – established by the first emperor, Augustus – was truly religious or rather, in practical terms, a secular political institution (Price, Simon, *Rituals*

- The banquet in 'Conspiracy' sees everyone seated at a long horseshoe table. Director Christopher Barry knew this was inaccurate. He says in the audio commentary:

  > 'This is the scene where there are so many of them sitting round, that they couldn't be **lying** around in the true Roman way, and we were criticised for putting them in chairs.'[93]

  Wealthy Romans – and none were more wealthy than the emperor – ate in recline, on *klinai* (nascent chaise lounges). They did this to flaunt their status; the manifest impracticality of it set apart those who could afford slaves to cut and serve each morsel[94]. Aptly enough, **Doctor Who**'s budget didn't stretch this far. The decadence portrayed was therefore more generic; more mediaeval than Roman.

- The 'Conspiracy' cliffhanger sees Ian bested in a gladiatorial match. The incidental music stops abruptly. 'Cut off his head!' Nero decrees, and gives a bloodthirsty thumbs-down. This is a pet peeve of Roman scholars. Social media has cemented our understanding of thumbs-up (positive) and thumbs-down (negative), yet these connotations are in fact relatively modern. In Ancient Rome the thumbs-down

---

and Power: The Roman Imperial Cult in Asia Minor, pp15-16), it would seem terribly unwise for Tavius, a slave of the imperial palace, to have kept about his person an icon that identified him as Christian.

[93] 'Conspiracy'.

[94] Roller, Matthew, 'Posture and Sex in the Roman *Convivium*', 55-59, in Gold, Barbara K., and John F. Donahue, eds, *Roman Dining*.

(pressed into a closed fist) was the gesture for sparing a gladiator. This is attested by medallion pictures and inscriptions[95]. The thumbs-up, conversely, was the cultural equivalent of today's raised middle finger[96]. This is one instance where *The Romans* could have done better: it would not only have been more accurate for Derek Francis to have given a boggle-eyed thumbs-up, but would also have tapped into the modern misconstruing and made him seem gleefully deranged.

Doctor Who to this extent distorts our understanding of the past. To reiterate, though: these historical infelicities aren't greatly important. What gaffes we see in *The Romans* (if we are uncharitable enough to call them such) were by and large the corollaries of dramatic licence and devil-driven necessity. Where the detail is erroneous, still the impression is more or less commensurate; and as we shall see, the past is too much of a battlefield already for us to waste time quibbling over the odd fact cast to the wayside...

---

[95] Corbeill, Anthony, *Nature Embodied: Gesture in Ancient Rome*, p8.
[96] Fabry, Merrill, 'Where Does the 'Thumbs-Up' Gesture Really Come From?' It seems the thumbs-up as an expression of 'all's well' was introduced by British soldiers during the First World War, then popularised by their American counterparts throughout the Second World War. The topsy-turvy retrofitting onto Roman times came about by way of a famous painting by Jean-Léon Gérôme: *Pollice Verso* ('Turned Thumb'), 1872, depicting the cruel baying of a gladiatorial crowd, vividly misinterpreting the Latin to show a sea of thumbs (in effect, turned wrists) pointed down, rather than thumbs unsheathed (turned up) from closed fists.

Ultimately, be it in textbooks or on television on a Saturday evening, history is whatever we choose to make of it.

CHAPTER 8: *THE ROMANS* AND COUNTERCULTURE – REWRITING THE MARGINS

From a 21st-century perspective, **Doctor Who**'s historical episodes offer two overlapping views of the past. The first of these is the strictly factual depiction; in this case, Neronian Rome in all its (vain)glory. The second is a cultural palimpsest thereof; in other words, that same Rome filtered through the milieu of the mid-1960s.

For all its educational remit, *The Romans* did not – could not – present Rome purely as the sum of Dennis Spooner's, Christopher Barry's, costume designer Daphne Dare's, and designer Raymond Cusick's historical knowledge. Leaving aside practical considerations of age-appropriate content, time and budget, the contemporary zeitgeist must also have left its mark upon production. Just as the Doctor, Barbara, Ian and Vicki brought their own preconceptions with them to Ancient Rome, so too must some flavour of the 1960s have seeped through.

The BBC at this time was still very much the instrument of a conservative Establishment, yet the making of **Doctor Who**, from Producer Verity Lambert down, was entrusted to up-and-comers who lived in Swinging London and whose time away from work inevitably would have exposed them to the rise of counterculture[97].

---

[97] London began swinging circa August 1963, the propagation of Mod culture – the music- and fashion-based British take on American youth culture – occurring thereafter at an unprecedented rate thanks in part to ITV's new live music programme **Ready,**

This inherent duality – an entwining of the staid traditionalist and the hip progressive[98] – is introduced within five minutes of **Doctor Who**'s first episode when Susan, standing for both the teenager and the alien, is seen listening to pop music on a transistor radio[99]. Ian and Barbara react with droll forbearance; what they are witnessing is not a threat to their worldview but rather the foibles of a 15-year-old schoolgirl.

In reality, of course, their worldview very much is endangered. Barbara and Ian – conceived as ordinary schoolteachers; identification figures who might serve as beaux idéals of post-war Britain[100] – are about to be abducted on a strange and harrowing adventure through time and space; an eye-opening ordeal from which all they crave is an end and thence a return to their old lives. Viewed as a product of Establishment television, **Doctor Who** was merely escapism for the young; an outlandish dream to be grown

---

Steady, Go! (Levy, Shawn, *Ready, Steady, Go! Swinging London and the Invention of Cool*, pp8, 120.) The global counterculture of the 1960s is said to have kicked off in earnest – in America at least – following the assassination of President Kennedy in November 1963. While America and England bounced revolutionary ideas off each other, **Doctor Who** in its formative years ran to a backdrop of social upheaval.

[98]'When Verity talked to me about the part, part of the attraction was that this was to be a sort of revolution, in a sense, in the BBC. This was to be the Young Turks who were going to take over.' (William Russell, 'Conspiracy' audio commentary).

[99] 'An Unearthly Child'.

[100] Originally as Miss Lola McGovern ('Timid but capable of sudden rabbit courage. Modest, with plenty of normal desires.') and Cliff ('Physically perfect, strong and courageous, a gorgeous dish.') ('"Dr Who" – General Notes on Background and Approach').

out of. Viewed in the context of counterculture, it was part of the subversion.

A counterculture, loosely defined, is any subculture whose values and practices stand in opposition to mainstream society. Some of history's more famous subcultures concerned themselves with freedom of expression: romanticism, bohemianism, the hippie movement. Such countercultures moved deliberately away from the mainstream, whereas others – those founded on a belief in personal equality – started apart but aimed to be included. These were the subcultures now associated with identity politics: those of race and class, gender, sexuality, and religion[101]. These politically conscious subcultures found new voice in the 1960s and, drawing strength from each other, gained collective impetus as **the** counterculture.

With due deference to artistic, hedonistic and intellectually minded subcultures, it is this more worldly counterculture of equality that holds our interest today (in no small part because its ideals are yet to be fully realised). To what extent did the burgeoning social consciousness of the mid-1960s manifest in **Doctor Who**'s portrayal of Ancient Rome in 64 CE? How compatible were London's values – both old and new – with those of Nero's Rome?

Race and Class

In a better world, issues of race and class would demand separate and distinct analyses. Given, however, the social makeup of London in the early to mid-1960s, and of Rome in Nero's time, there seems

---

[101] To these we might (and with reference to *The Romans*, will) add impairment and disability.

valid reason to view these particular subcultures as being substantially overlapping.

Doctor Who was born into a society where racism was endemic; where the white English majority, regardless of class, thought itself if not inherently superior to the various coloured and non-English white minorities, then certainly more entitled to be there. These other peoples formed a conceptual underclass, which rarely saw any representation on conservative BBC television, let alone one that was favourable.

As shown in *An Unearthly Child*, Coal Hill School looks to be middle class and exclusively white[102]. Whether or not this segregation is historically accurate, it was acknowledged and in some measure apologised for in *Remembrance of the Daleks* (1988), which returned to the same time period and, though again representing the students as white, elsewhere drew critical attention to the racial prejudice[103].

The British Empire may have been in (escalating) decline after the Second World War, yet in **Doctor Who**'s early years an empire it remained, and at its heart lay conservative white London. This is where we first encounter the Doctor, and, Susan's dancing

---

[102] Wood and Miles identify Coal Hill, though having the characteristics of a comprehensive school (which in 1963 would be an anachronism), as being either a 'superior secondary modern' or 'very lax grammar' school under the Tripartite System in operation at that time (Wood and Miles, *About Time* #1 p17).

[103] The skewed demographic then was subjected to reform in the **Doctor Who** spinoff **Class** (2016), whose 21st-century depiction proves as much a flagship for inclusion as early **Doctor Who** was a perpetuator of non-mainstream invisibility.

notwithstanding, it is not until the end of season 3 – *The War Machines* (1966) – that the programme begins overtly to acknowledge (and thence countenance) ways of life that aren't both Establishment-regulated and performed by actors trained in Received Pronunciation.

The Romans predates this broadening of perspective. Hence, it is not the cockney sailor Ben and the hip, liberated Polly who travel back to Ancient Rome; it is Barbara and Ian (paragons of the post-war British Empire), Vicki (whose teenage insouciance is more age-related than countercultural), and of course the Doctor (a Victorian-style gentleman and the self-righteous embodiment of white privilege)[104]. Beneath the surface of its comedy-adventure, *The Romans* is essentially the clash of two dominant discourses; of two great empires, each of which at its peak accounted for upwards of one-fifth of the world population.

Despite the vastness of the Roman Empire – or perhaps because of it – the social order in Nero's time was heavily Rome-centric. At the top was the Emperor, then the senators and the equestrians (two strata of a wealthy, property-owning elite), ordinary Roman citizens, freedmen (that is, former slaves who became junior members of the family that had owned them), foreigners, and lastly the slaves. The lowliness of slaves, however, was in practice not so clear. Because they were property, their owners' status had to be taken into account; likewise freedmen, who legally ranked below regular citizens but more judiciously might be treated in accordance with

---

[104] See, for example, Fly, Fire, 'The White Doctor', and Hernandez, Mike, '"You can't just change what I look like without consulting me!"' in Orthia, Lindy, ed, *Doctor Who and Race*.

their new families' eminence[105]. Effectively, then, this positioned foreigners most precariously within the social order. Romanness was all-important[106]. Non-Roman citizens in Rome formed the same sort of conceptual underclass as did the non-whites and non-English of London.

Having crashed the TARDIS, the Doctor, Ian, Barbara and Vicki begin 'The Slave Traders' luxuriating at a villa just north of the capital. Given Ian's misgivings about staying too long ('The owner of this house could come back') and then his reaction when they are discovered ('We... can explain'), it seems clear that they are there without permission. The owner, Flavius Giscard, is off fighting in Gaul; and though the stallholder assumes the Doctor and company are friends of his, we may conclude instead that they have taken vacant possession, or have imperiously talked their way past household slaves[107].

This appropriation of Empire – the presumptuous sense of entitlement – shows not just in their moving in and taking what they want, but also in their choice of clothing. Whereas the Romans

---

[105] Matyszak, Philip, *Ancient Rome on Five Denarii a Day*, pp57-59.

[106] Non-Romans couldn't even marry into citizenship. The only way was to become a citizen's slave and subsequently, trusting them to keep their word, a freedman (Matyszak, *Ancient Rome on Five Denarii a Day* p58).

[107] None of whom appears in the serial. The seeming desertedness of the villa (save for the time travellers) is inexplicable from a plot perspective but no doubt was expedient in terms of production. When Ian and Barbara return there at daybreak in 'Inferno', Ian notes, 'If the master was back, the servants would be [up].' This, however, gives no clear indication of whether or not there were household slaves present (if unseen) in 'The Slave Traders'.

in day-to-day life would wear tunics[108], the time travellers are dressed more formally: Vicki in a stola; Barbara in a cross between a stola and a toga (the latter of which would identify her either as a 1960s Briton with grandiose notions, or as a prostitute); Ian in a toga (which, since he wasn't a Roman citizen, would be illegal for him to wear); and the Doctor in a rich, gaudy ensemble that could easily have belonged to the emperor himself[109]. Formal Roman attire was notoriously uncomfortable; that the 1960s British imperials chose it for lounging purposes suggests either the need to fool somebody (again, the servants?) or that they were making a game – an inherently condescending game – of going native.

The other explanation, of course, is that Dare, Spooner and Barry simply got it wrong (or intentionally fed an ignorant audience what it expected)[110]. Error would also account for Flavius Giscard's absence campaigning in Gaul – and for the influx of slaves from there – over a hundred years after Julius Caesar had finished subduing this region. (It should be noted that Albert Uderzo got the clothing right in the **Asterix** comics which appeared in France around the same time as *The Romans*[111], and showed the same attention to detail when drawing Rome as a thriving, cosmopolitan

---

[108] Matyszak, *Ancient Rome on Five Denarii a Day* pp36-38.

[109] The people at the marketplace are less well-attired, as are the attendees of Nero's banquet, although from a production standpoint this no doubt reflects the policy of spending money where it would be most on show.

[110] The latter being justification, apparently, for much of the historical inaccuracy in Ridley Scott's *Gladiator* (2000).

[111] In Goscinny, René, and Albert Uderzo, *Asterix the Gladiator*, for instance, which was first serialised in 1962 and then collated in 1964.

metropolis, the heart of a mighty and racially diverse empire.)

In keeping with the BBC's penchant for homogeneous Anglicising, the most notable aspect of racial diversity in *The Romans* is that there isn't any. Ethnically, the Gallic slaves look just like the Romans, who in turn look just like the time-travelling Britons; and if any foreigners have come to Rome from elsewhere in the Empire – modern day Portugal, Spain, Germany, Greece, Turkey, Syria, Egypt, Libya – well, then they bear an equally uncanny resemblance to the retrofitted Imperial standard. Just as the production glossed over the complexities of Rome's class system, so too did it ignore issues of race... with one exception.

In 55 and 54 BCE, Julius Caesar had invaded but not conquered Britain, and it was only in 43 CE that the Emperor Claudius added Britain to the Roman Empire. London itself was not established until sometime around 50 CE, and during Nero's reign was but a tiny settlement. Nonetheless, when the slaver Didius overhears Barbara and Vicki talk of being from Londinium, he recognises it ('The town they spoke of is in a place they call Britannia') and the other slaver, Sevcheria, is coolly satisfied ('They are Britons; perfect'). The time travellers' complacent assumption of superiority is then shown to be false. Ian and Barbara are abducted and enslaved. They are no longer members of a privileged elite, but rather foreigners a long way from home; and Rome in 64 CE could be every bit as abusive of outsiders as London was in the 1960s.

The Doctor, too, has his presupposed superiority subverted. Impersonating a lyre player from Corinth, he casts himself as Greek (and Vicki presumably as his slave). This might make him a better class of foreigner than the newly conquered Britons, yet still his situation is perilous. He places himself entirely at the merciless whim of a mad emperor, **and is too self-assured even to realise**. This last part, of course, is a product of the comedy (just as Barbara and Ian's enslavement is a product of the drama); yet the effect is to demonstrate the ingrained arrogance of empire. The Doctor and Nero jostle for supremacy, each oblivious to even the possibility of coming off second-best. The same blind confidence could be attributed to the British and Roman Empires.

Sexuality

The historical record paints Nero as sexually depraved. In addition to his many liaisons with mistresses and slaves (both male and female), he is said to have maintained an incestuous relationship with his mother[112], to have sexually abused his young step-brother Britannicus[113], to have raped a Vestal Virgin[114], to have instituted sex resorts and pop-up brothels (in which married women were forced to serve)[115], and to have practised bondage and genital mutilation on unwilling men, women and children[116].

Casual brutality aside, this is not how Nero is portrayed in *The Romans*.

Two obvious caveats emerge: firstly, that **Doctor Who** was intended

---

[112] Suetonius, *Nero*, 28; Tacitus, *Annals*, 14.2. As per convention in studying ancient history, primary sources are herein cited according to their own internal numbering systems, not with reference to any particular modern edition.
[113] Tacitus, *Annals*, 13.17.
[114] Suetonius, *Nero*, 28.
[115] Tacitus, *Annals*, 15.37.
[116] Suetonius, *Nero*, 29.

primarily as children's television and so could not possibly show the extent of Nero's deviance; secondly, that *The Romans* was an experiment in comedy, which ruled out a full account of the Emperor's sadism[117].

History, of course, can be fickle. Ultimately, we've no way of knowing whether Nero did those things the ancient writers Tacitus, Cassius Dio, Suetonius, et al attribute to him[118]. On the other hand, we can probably say with some confidence that he didn't conduct himself in the manner written by Dennis Spooner and played by Derek Francis. On the balance of probabilities, Nero was far more likely an unchecked sexual predator than an impish objectifier of women and purveyor of 'naughty' British fantasies.

Nero's sexual behaviour has been toned down in *The Romans*, and no doubt there was good reason for this; but what of his inclinations? The historical Nero was bisexual at least – quite possibly pansexual[119] – yet in **Doctor Who** there is no indication that he is anything other than heterosexual. What of his desire for men and boys? Granted, the latter could play no part in a serial

---

[117] Also, *The Romans* shows only one or two days in Nero's life; he couldn't have been indulging his lust all the time.

[118] Champlin, Edward, *Nero*, pp161-62, for instance, leans towards the belief that he did not.

[119] In 64 CE Nero married the freedman Pythagoras, with Nero acting as wife (Tacitus, *Annals*, 15.37); in 66 CE he then became husband to another freedman, Sporus (Cassius Dio LXII.28). Champlin, however, questions Nero's adopting the passive sexual role vis-à-vis Pythagoras, alleging deliberate misrepresentation re this and also Nero's supposed genital mutilations (Champlin, *Nero* pp166-69).

being broadcast at 5.40 on a Saturday evening. But through much of *The Romans* Nero is attended by Tigilinus, a non-speaking comedy character who in real life Tacitus says 'perverted Nero to every kind of atrocity'[120]. The silencing of Tigilinus could be another coincidence – another by-product of the comedy – yet in the context of BBC Establishment values it could equally be an act of calculated significance.

In 1954 the British government established a committee to consider the laws in respect to homosexual offences and prostitution. In 1957 this committee delivered its findings – the Wolfenden Report – and recommended the decriminalising of homosexual acts between consenting adults. Although the Wolfenden Report has been criticised for not actively valuing the homosexual subculture[121], its publication nevertheless was an important event in the fight for gay rights. Even so, it wasn't until the Sexual Offences Act 1967 that homosexual activity was (at least partially) decriminalised in England. That a decade passed between the Wolfenden Report and the Sexual Offences Act can be attributed at least in part to outspoken opposition from the Establishment[122]. Given such vehement condemnation levelled by the upright and

---

[120] Tacitus, *Histories*, 1.72. According to Cassius Dio LXII.15, Tigellinus (the spelling is different but it seems beyond coincidence that Spooner chose this particular name) organised the banquet-cum-wandering-debauchery wherein Nero and his companions roamed the city, defiling any woman or girl whom they chose, regardless of her status.

[121] Higgins, Patrick, *Heterosexual Dictatorship*, p89.

[122] Even those who spoke in favour of reforming the law adamantly maintained their opposition to homosexuality itself. See *Sexual Offences Bill*, HL Deb 16 June 1966 vol 275 cc146-77.

privileged, perhaps it is little wonder that **Doctor Who** limited Nero's licentiousness to heterosexual hanky-panky.

In 1936 director Josef von Sternberg embarked upon a film version of Robert Graves' novel *I, Claudius*. The motion picture was never completed, but in a 1965 documentary about it, *The Epic That Never Was*, actor Emlyn Williams talks about how von Sternberg wanted him to play Nero:

> 'I was introduced to him [von Sternberg] and he took me aside [...] and said, "This part, you know, is a very cruel, degenerate man," and I said, "Yes, I see that." He said, "Perhaps so degenerate, perhaps a little bit sissy; not too much".'[123]

Here lies an interesting dichotomy: between conservative distaste – the instinct to have Nero's nonconformist sexuality swept under the carpet – and an appreciation of shock value; that is, invoking effeminacy as a telltale to further proclivities for which Nero might be demonised.

It could be argued that the **Doctor Who** production aimed for a similar juxtaposition: underplaying the crueller aspects of Nero's libidinous excesses while at the same time using the caprices of farce to hint at more wicked debaucheries. Given, though, the public debate sparked by the Wolfenden Report, and thence the increased public mindfulness of homosexuality in the early to mid-1960s, it remains more than plausible that the heterosexualising of Nero was a considered act of subcultural suppression.

---

[123] *The Epic That Never Was*, 20m 20s to 20m 40s.

The devil's advocate might suggest at this point that any normalising of Nero was, if not a boon, then at least a kindness to the sexual minority. It distanced them from a historical personage who, irrespective of his sexuality, was negatively perceived. Notwithstanding broader issues of censorship and exclusion, where this contention most obviously falls down is that Nero in *The Romans* is given a sympathetic treatment. He is the villain, yes, but also the star of the programme's unfolding comedy. Young viewers would not have known of Nero's bisexuality, but adults could easily have come across it by way of the Hollywood blockbuster *Quo Vadis* (1951), in which Peter Ustinov portrays the emperor as 'mincingly epicene, precious, displaying large elements of stereotyped effeteness and coded homosexuality'[124]. By removing Nero's bisexuality alongside his more egregious sex crimes, **Doctor Who** tacitly includes bisexuality as one of those crimes.

Ten years on, **The Goodies** would redress the sexual balance in the BBC's comedic representation of Nero with *Rome Antics* (1975), in which Roy Kinnear played a wonderfully camp emperor whose interest in Bill Oddie's character is surpassed only by his fetish for fruit. A year after that, the BBC also made progress on the dramatic front with **I, Claudius** (1976), a star-studded 12-episode adaptation, the final instalment of which (*Old King Log*) saw Christopher Biggins embody Nero with self-possessed, primped effeminacy. A decade after *The Romans*, the BBC thus showed that, creatively speaking, it could retain Nero's bisexuality within both a comedic and a historical character study, albeit in programmes first broadcast at

---

[124] Babington, Bruce, and Peter William Evans, *Biblical Epics*, p204.

9pm[125]. In 1965, on children's television and when the prevailing ideology carried more than a strong dose of homophobia, **Doctor Who** steered well clear.

Gender

The year 1963 saw the assassination of President Kennedy (22 November), the beginning of **Doctor Who** (23 November), and two other events of long-reaching significance and effect: the publication of Betty Friedan's book *The Feminine Mystique* (19 February), and the release of *American Women* (11 October); that is, the findings of the Presidential Commission on the Status of Women (established by Kennedy's executive order on 14 December 1961). These two trigger points gave rise to the movement we know as second-wave feminism[126].

Where first-wave feminists fought for suffrage – that vital first step towards equality – second-wave feminists took their fight into the workplace and the home, seeking recognition of women's (often suppressed or repudiated) capabilities, and thence equality of pay and opportunity, and an end to domestic pigeonholing. The tides of history have since given rise to third- and fourth-wave feminism, yet the objectives of the second wave, even today, remain some way from being realised. In the early years of **Doctor Who** they must have seemed very distant indeed.

---

[125] Although *Rome Antics* originally went out at this time (on BBC2, 7 April 1975), the repeat screening was considerably earlier, at 6.50pm (on BBC1, 13 October 1975) (Pixley, Andrew, *The Goodies*, p564).

[126] Or at least the facet of second-wave feminism concerned with liberal equality (Evans, Judith, *Feminist Theory Today*, p13).

Verity Lambert was 27 years old when she took the job as **Doctor Who**'s first Producer, becoming in doing so the BBC's youngest overall and only female Producer of drama[127]. Unmarried and career-driven, forging her own path in a male-dominated industry, she was in many ways the embodiment of the successful self-determinism that second-wave feminism advocated. Whether or not Lambert was actively committed to the cause, her example would in and of itself have been sufficient to instil in her male colleagues a greater mindfulness of gender representation.

LM Myles, in her critique of *The Ambassadors of Death* (1970), devotes an insightful chapter to the paucity of female acknowledgement in 1970s **Doctor Who**, writing: 'Before the '80s if there are even three speaking roles given to women in a story, then it gets a small cheer from me.'[128]

The Romans rises above this (tellingly low) benchmark. Barbara is joined by Vicki, who in this early story is a more independent, more wilful character than Susan had become. In addition to the two regulars, *The Romans* also gives us the Empress Poppaea (Kay Patrick) and the poisoner Locusta (Ann Tirard), both of whom have small but significant roles; and then the stallholder (Margot Thomas) and the woman slave (Dorothy-Rose Gribble), bringing the tally of speaking parts to six. Furthermore, unlike *The Ambassadors of Death* where Myles can take only cold comfort from the one scene that has an equal number of men and women on screen[129], *The Romans* on several occasions affords significant screen time to

---

[127] BBC News, 'Doctor Who's First Producer Dies'.
[128] Myles, LM, *The Black Archive #3, The Ambassadors of Death* p57.
[129] Myles, *The Ambassadors of Death* p59.

women interacting without any male presence: Barbara and Vicki ('The Slave Traders'); Barbara, Vicki and the stall holder ('The Slave Traders'); Barbara and the slave woman ('All Roads Lead to Rome'); Barbara and Poppaea ('Conspiracy'); Vicki and Locusta ('Conspiracy'); and Poppaea and Locusta ('Conspiracy').

But how flattering were these roles? Our devil's advocate might argue that the guest parts are all negative: Poppaea, the jealous wife; Locusta, a poisoner without conscience; the grasping, sourly disposed stall holder who dooms Barbara and Ian to slavery; and the dirty, wretched, dying slave woman. Only Vicki shows any real sign of feminist progressiveness, while Barbara, for all the dignity with which Jacqueline Hill plays her, remains at the mercy of a male-dominated world. The women in the story may have been apportioned more of the script than was common – more of the dialogue – but does this greater exposure do them justice? Can the promotion of women in *The Romans* be seen as counterculture at work, or is it merely an aberrational consequence of Spooner's divide-and-comedify storyline?

For a true appreciation of the gender representation, we have to consider the historical contrast between women in post-suffragette London and women in Ancient Rome. Yes, second-wave feminism might only have been in its early stages when *The Romans* was made. Yes, Rome by some measures was a great civilisation. But where women in the 1960s were striding with purpose on the long road to equality, the women of Ancient Rome were still legally the property of their male relatives. Their rights, from any meaningful perspective, weren't just a far cry from the feminist ideal; they were non-existent.

Market stalls in Ancient Rome were run by both women and men. The stallholder in *The Romans* could have been either, but was cast as a woman. This, despite her negative portrayal, must be considered a positive step. (In answer to the devil's advocate we should note that negative portrayals are very much the norm in *The Romans*; of all the period characters, only one – Delos – is depicted as being unambiguously good[130].) Slaves, likewise, could be of either sex. The slave that Barbara helps may have been written as female so as to accentuate Barbara's charitable nature (an important plot point), yet in this sense the woman slave's abject condition – which in any case is a reflection on her captors, not her – is the essential flipside of showing a modern woman to have superior morals to those of ancient men.

Whereas the stallholder and the slave were generic characters, Poppaea and Locusta were real historical figures. According to the ancient sources, it was through Poppaea's manipulation that Nero had both his first wife and then his mother murdered[131]. Her attempted poisoning of Barbara is thus consistent with actual history, albeit that in **Doctor Who** her motivation comes across more as jealousy than ambition. What is most notable about Poppaea in *The Romans* is that, although imperious and ruthless, she calls upon her negative attributes out of necessity in dealing with her wayward husband. Here we see a woman with no legal standing and no formal power managing through sheer force of personality to keep a capricious madman in fear and awe of her. It is

---

[130] Even the doddering old lyre player Maximus Pettulian is, it transpires, an assassin sent to do Nero in.
[131] Tacitus, *Annals*, 14.1, 14.61-64.

a pre-feminist tour de force.

In addition to the speaking cast, director Christopher Barry[132] ensured that women can be seen in the background wherever it was historically plausible: at the marketplace and amongst the Gallic slaves ('The Slave Traders'); in the crowd at the slave market ('All Roads Lead to Rome'); and at Nero's court and during the banquet ('Conspiracy'). This was not necessarily the product of affirmative action – an assiduous pursuit of realism would have produced the same effect – but even if Barry's support is not proven, writer Dennis Spooner does for one seem actively to have promoted female representation.

The final word on this must go to Locusta. In the historical record, Locusta is a shadowy figure whom Nero called upon to poison Britannicus[133]. In *The Romans* she works in the open and describes herself proudly as 'Official poisoner to the court of Caesar Nero.' The notion is faintly absurd; yet while it could have been introduced for comic effect, there's no noticeable sense of this. Through Locusta we see instead counterculture at work: in 1960s Ancient Rome – that is, not in historical truth but as filtered through the new ideals of second-wave feminism – a woman's expertise could be recognised and valued.

---

[132] Or more practically, perhaps, production assistant David Maloney ('Conspiracy' audio commentary).
[133] Suetonius, *Nero*, 33. Locusta had previously been employed by Nero's mother to prepare a poison for his predecessor, the emperor Claudius (Tacitus, *Annals*, 12.66).

Religion

The most puzzling character in *The Romans* is Tavius, who, acting as Nero's major-domo, purchases Barbara at the slave auction. Tavius is party to a conspiracy against the emperor. He vexes the Doctor with his unintelligible tête-à-têtes on the matter, then is revealed at the last to be a Christian, who helps Barbara flee the palace. Indeed, he brought Barbara there in the first place to keep her safe, recognising in her a kindly person with (to retrofit the notion) good Christian morals. This despite participating himself in a plot to kill the emperor, and knowing the inevitable turmoil that would follow.

What is going on?

Tavius represents the ambivalent mystery element of *The Romans*. We only recognise him as a Christian in 'Inferno' when he gazes out the window to where Barbara is escaping and the camera zooms in on the cross he's fingering, with Tavius murmuring, 'Good luck, my child. Good luck.' None of this makes immediate sense. Indeed, we could easily dismiss it as a muddled sub-plot with no wider implications. But let's delve a little deeper.

The Romans ends with the Great Fire of Rome, the event with which Nero is most notoriously – if perhaps erroneously – associated. Though absent from Rome at the time, Nero was vilified in public opinion and so looked to shift the blame... to the Christians[134]. Though ineffective in deflecting the rumours, his 'reprisals' against the Christians were brutal. Tacitus writes:

'Covered with the skins of beasts, they were torn by dogs

---

[134] Griffin, *Nero* pp132-33.

and perished, or were nailed to crosses, or were doomed to the flames and burnt, to serve as a nightly illumination, when daylight had expired.'[135]

Religion in the Roman Empire was pantheist but inclusive, yet the Christians were a distinct minority and, as Tacitus puts it, 'a class hated for their abominations'[136]. Although it remains difficult to reconcile Tavius' complicity in an assassination plot, his behaviour vis-à-vis Barbara seems a deliberate contrast with that of Nero, and thus an assertion of Christian righteousness.

This becomes particularly noteworthy in light of the religious counterculture of the 'long 1960s'[137], whereby the hegemony of the Christian churches was on the wane, the national identity making room for the existence of other faiths (or non-faiths) and thence giving way eventually to secularism[138]. Upon the publication, for instance, of the controversial non-fiction bestseller *Honest to God* on 1 December 1963 – written by John AT Robinson (then Bishop of Woolwich) in advocacy of secular theology – the conservative Establishment, challenged now on all fronts, might well have thrown its hands up and lamented, 'Is nothing sacred?'

In *The Romans*, we are presented with a religious majority under threat – Christianity in the 1960s – making a play for public approbation by showing an earlier, minority form of itself that was

---

[135] Tacitus, *Annals*, 15.44.
[136] Tacitus, *Annals*, 15.44.
[137] 1958-74. McLeod, Hugh, *The Religious Crisis of the 1960s*, p1 (citing Marwick, Arthur, *The Sixties: Cultural Revolution in Britain, France, Italy and the United States c1958-1974* p7).
[138] McLeod, *The Religious Crisis of the 1960s* p2.

known to have been unjustly persecuted. In **Doctor Who** terms, this is the subtextual equivalent of a multi-Doctor story where the haughty, self-important current incarnation, in times of extraordinary crisis, is teamed up with a predecessor whose help is to be grudgingly accepted even while its giver is looked down upon[139].

Impairment, Disability and Handicap

Given that the counterculture of the 1960s arose in opposition to a prescriptive, normative Establishment, it is unsurprising that it incorporated a greater appreciation of the mentally ill – people who thought differently – and thence of impairment in general[140]. Unfortunately, this rethinking is not evident in *The Romans*.

The assassin Ascaris has had his tongue cut out. As the Doctor chirpily elucidates to Vicki: 'My dear, it was an accepted thing in this age to hire an assassin. Preferably someone dumb, and then he couldn't denounce you.'[141]

This explanation is helpful only insofar as it reveals a prejudice. The Doctor propagates the nonsensical concept – seen most famously in Shakespeare's *Titus Andronicus* – that a person without speech cannot communicate effectively; cannot testify. In Roman times, until the Emperor Justinian's legal reforms of 529 and 565 CE there

---

[139] *The Three Doctors* (1972-73) began this trend, and it was seen most recently in *Twice Upon a Time*, albeit the first Doctor in this latter instance is invoked less to help the 12th, per se, than subtextually by Steven Moffat to prepare the way for the 13th.
[140] Rovito, Maria R, *Disability and Mental Illness in 1960s Countercultural Literature*, pp6-7.
[141] 'All Roads Lead to Rome'.

was a law prohibiting deaf and deaf-mute persons from giving testimony[142], but this, though still closed-minded, was predicated on how reliably an eye-witness could take receipt of information, not deliver it.

Ascaris is not deaf, and there is no historical basis for linking his impairment with his profession. Nor is his disability portrayed in such a manner as to suggest that Dennis Spooner or Christopher Barry had inclusiveness or counterculture in mind. Indeed, the scripting (or directing) of Ascaris as a figure of ridicule is, fair to say, *The Romans'* one true failing, and one that is in no way corrected on the DVD audio commentary.

When Ascaris is interrogated by the centurion, his would-be-comedic speechlessness provokes a general expression of mirth in the commentary booth. Barry Jackson, who played Ascaris, far from regretting the performance he had to give, takes the bad joke even further by associating not only Ascaris' muteness and incompetence but also William Hartnell's arteriosclerosis-induced botching of lines. He says to William Russell:

> 'And of course you used to tell a story about when he [William Hartnell] had so much dialogue to say, and he used to go, "What? What?" if he dried, and you used to help him out. But of course with me it was no hope, because he'd go, "What? What?" and I'd just go, "Urrr..."'[143]

Though in bad taste, again this anecdote reduces the commentators

---

[142] Preuss, Julius, *Biblical and Talmudic Medicine*, p292 (citing Dernburg, *Pandekten*, Vol 3: 129).
[143] 'The Slave Traders'.

to guffaws.

A curious echo of Ascaris arises in the season 3 story *The Myth Makers*. Although the following is difficult to verify – the BBC having wiped its master copy, only the audio recordings and some still shots remain – it seems that *The Myth Makers*, like *The Romans*, made ill use of an impaired character. Writer Donald Cotton recollects:

> 'The title of one of the episodes was greeted with bared gums at one script conference – I think it may have been "Is There a Doctor in the Horse?" – so a bright apprentice suggested "Death of a Spy" as a more suitable alternative. At this I pointed out that the plot contained no spy, and therefore his death would be difficult to arrange. They urged me to include one, and have him killed – why not use Tutte Lemkow, who was anyway under contract? "No time," I said. "Dialogue all written and plot constructed to fill 25 minutes." "Then let's make him a deaf mute, so that he won't take up any time and won't need lines," they argued. I reeled in disbelief while they did exactly that – and if you saw the episode, you may have wondered why my friend Tutte flitted pointlessly about the action, looking sinister and confused, under the strange billing of 'Cyclops'. **That** is entirely why!!'[144]

There's a good chance here that Cotton was setting the record crooked as much as straight, piqued perhaps by the substitution of

---

[144] David Auger, ghost-written from discussions with Donald Cotton. Reproduced in Walker, Stephen James, *Talkback* p117.

episode titles.[145] Nonetheless, *The Romans* and *The Myth Makers*, despite having different directors, writers, Script Editors and Producers, did both make light of impairment. Ascaris' (almost bestial) unintelligibility is suggestive of a link between muteness and lack of intellect. Likewise, in 'Death of a Spy', Steven talks very slowly to Cyclops, as if some associative mental impairment must lurk behind the other's grunting responses[146]. Was this denigration within comedy justified? While recognising that a programme should not be condemned for being of its time, nevertheless we might question the approach.

By definition, counterculture seeks to redress mainstream attitudes; and since the unimpaired majority had for so long held impairment as a fit subject for mockery, it is little wonder that television comedies of the 1960s carried this attitude forward: from the care-related plot machinations of **Steptoe and Son** to the comic belittling of characters such as Albert Riddle, the one-armed dishwasher of **Robin's Nest** (1977-81)[147], and onwards to the present day. The Ancient Romans themselves took cruel delight in impairment, their

---

[145] As Wood and Miles point out, 'Death of a Spy', though less funny than 'Is There a Doctor in the Horse?', would have carried more dramatic clout as a tune-in-next-week teaser leading out of the previous episode ('Small Prophet, Quick Return'), where Cassandra has just denounced Vicki as a spy and demanded she be put to death (Wood and Miles, *About Time* #1, p202). The surviving storyline for the episode also includes the presence of Cyclops, which would seem to contradict Cotton's version (*The Complete History* volume 6, p77).
[146] In the script, Cyclops has had his tongue cut out, and only has one eye. There is no suggestion, however, that he is deaf.
[147] Clark, 'Disabling Comedy', pp10, 3.

mythology going so far as to have a deformed god (Vulcan) scorned by all the others[148]. But even if the humour was historically apt and the counterculture of the 1960s slow to take hold, there still seems little reason to make Ascaris impaired. His function within the story – an assassin at work – renders him situationally mute anyway, and it is his **ineffectualness** that is funny. Notwithstanding that television audiences of 1965 may have been generally disposed to laugh at impairment and disability, Ascaris' gibbering stultification appears not only a gratuitous but also a rather superfluous use of the trope[149].

One satisfying turnaround with regards impairment in these early **Doctor Who** comedies is that, as a rewriter of history, Donald Cotton managed the last laugh. When novelising *The Myth Makers* in 1985, he took the 'Cyclops' character and turned him into the epic poet Homer, thereupon narrating the entire story from his perspective. In 1987 he did something similar with *The Romans*, crafting an epistolary novel in which Ascaris not only tells his side of the story (through letters home) but also survives his fight with the Doctor and goes on to play a not insignificant part in unfolding events. Bad things still happen to both Cyclops and Ascaris – anything less would be a denial of their treatment on screen – but through Cotton's novelisations each is recognised and given voice.

---

[148] For more on attitudes towards disability in Ancient Rome, see: Lodder, B, 'Are They Monsters or Entertainment?'.

[149] Tigilinus, in contrast, is also situationally mute and victimised for laughs as he attends the emperor; but he is not identified as being impaired.

CHAPTER 9: A VIEWER'S RESPONSE TO *THE ROMANS*

The Romans was an important story in the context of **Doctor Who**'s burgeoning longevity. History has judged it kindly. Yet for all its humour and for all that its experimentation had repercussions, it was at time of broadcast just four weekly instalments of a television show made under exacting circumstances; one more episodic adventure of a programme put together at frantic pace and airing on all but six Saturday nights of the year.

Much has been written about the limitations of **Doctor Who**'s budget and recording schedule, as well as the restrictions imposed by television production more generally in the 1960s. *The Romans* was not spared these constraints. It did, however, rise above them. Through script and direction, costume and design, music and sound and, above all, acting, *The Romans* aspired to – and for a large part achieved – a level of quality that sets it apart from many of **Doctor Who**'s 20th-century serials.

The Romans, like all of **Doctor Who** at the time, was made to be broadcast once and then sold overseas and forgotten about. What is most extraordinary about *The Romans*, then, is its rewatchability – an ungainly word, but germane. Unlike, for example, such Jon Pertwee epics as *Colony in Space* (1971) or *The Monster of Peladon* (1974), where seeing everything unfold again can be something of a chore, the craftsmanship of *The Romans* becomes more evident with repeat viewings. This was throwaway television, yet really, really good!

So why does it work so well?

What follows is a viewing critique of *The Romans*, which in deference to the four-part structure – and in particular the farcical nature of 'Conspiracy' – shall be conducted on an episode-by-episode basis, commencing with:

'The Slave Traders'

'The slave traders raid a peaceful villa, and Dr Who takes up the lyre.'

[*Radio Times* billing for 'The Slave Traders']

Direction

Christopher Barry, if we're being honest, starts off on the wrong foot. The TARDIS materialises teetering on a precipice and then, just **before** it goes over, the Doctor and company start falling about the console room. Their stumbling is too tumultuous to associate with the ship's gentle rocking, yet too restrained to match its subsequent plummet. (Note: there isn't even a sudden upward tilt of the camera; just a wilful ring-a-ring o' roses until they all sneeze and fall down.)

To be fair, staggering about and pretending to be off-balance later became a staple of **Doctor Who** console room scenes, and one that nobody executed with any real panache until the 21st century. Whatever Barry's failings at this early attempt, he soon comes into his own.

First, a bit of trickery: he zooms the camera in on the crashed TARDIS, then cuts to a close-up of Ian lying unconscious; only... a month has passed! Ian is not so much knocked out as in recline, savouring a bunch of grapes that's about to make its way into shot. Perhaps this sleight of hand is as much Dennis Spooner's as

Christopher Barry's — it is, after all, the sort of misdirection upon which the script often turns — but for the rest of the episode it is very much Barry pulling the strings.

He uses different camera angles to show the assassin Ascaris concealed in a depth of foliage. He cleverly introduces the lyre player Maximus Pettulian in the background at the marketplace, and times Barbara and Vicki's arrival perfectly to align with the conversation between slave traders Sevcheria and Didius.

For a programme that in later years would be plagued by a lack of movement, Christopher Barry allows his scenes to flow. The villa sequences are particularly good in this respect. Take for example the Chesterfield / Chesterton exchange (10m 30s to 10m 45s):

Shot #1:

[Front-on view of the table.]

DOCTOR

[Packs fruit into a bag while Ian approaches.]

I think these should last me two or three days, hmm?

IAN

[While Barbara stands up.]

You never told us you were going away.

DOCTOR

[While Barbara leaves with a tray.]

Oh? Well, I don't know that I was under any obligation to report my movements to you, Chesterfield.

BARBARA

[Turns around.]

Chester-**ton**.

DOCTOR

[Pausing to point to her.]

Oh, Barbara's calling to you.

Shot #2:

[Close-up.]

IAN

[Turns from the Doctor to Barbara.]

Shot #3:

[Side-on view of the Doctor and Vicki.]

VICKI

[Laughs.]

Another example is Ian's 'Friends! Romans! Countrymen!' speech:

Shot #1:

[Front-on view of Ian and Barbara, medium close. The camera stays on Ian as he walks away from Barbara, behind a column and back around into close-up.]

IAN

Friends! Romans! Countrymen! Lend me your ears. I come to bury Caesar…

[The camera stops tracking. Ian disappears from shot, revealing Barbara rolling her eyes at his continuing speech.]

IAN

...not to praise him.

In both instances Christopher Barry has taken what could have been static scenes and made them dynamic. The direction is very good by and of itself. Given that it was achieved with unwieldy studio cameras and on-the-fly vision editing – in time-poor recording conditions where retakes were reserved strictly for major gaffes – the graceful charm of these scenes is all the more telling.

Costume and Design

Barry's direction works at least in part because he has been given the social setting and space with which to pull it off, the former courtesy of Daphne Dare and the latter thanks to Ray Cusick.

Dare sets the scene early, dressing Ian and (particularly) the Doctor in luxuriant-looking Roman attire. She matches this with Barbara's and Vicki's dresses, the slave buyers' outfits (of which the leader, Sevcheria, receives the better), and rounds off the episode by decking out a shiny-looking centurion. The only character who looks short-shrifted by budget is poor old Ascaris, whose costume consists of a sack and some wristbands. However, this is in keeping with his low standing in an emerging hierarchy of power and charisma.

At this point in the serial, Cusick's design work is exemplary. The model TARDIS on the cliff's edge works well, as does the crashed Ship. The villa in which the Doctor and company are staying is utterly resplendent. The sense of opulence is very real, giving the viewer every reason to invest in this strange new notion of holidaying time travellers. The space of the set not only affords the script room to breathe; it lets the actors move around and even allows for a little gag when Ian wanders after the Doctor in one direction, only for him to have moved through unseen parts of the villa and appeared again from the other.

The road to the village is also quite believable – these were the glory days when **Doctor Who** could manage plant life in the studio – and the only criticism, if one were peevish enough to make it, might be that the marketplace is a little **too** grandiose for the village it represents!

Music and Sound

One of the first and most effective means by which *The Romans* is set apart from the preceding stories' continuous narrative is by the use of noise. We hear birdsong both inside the villa and, louder, on the road to the village. This is unobtrusive yet markedly effectual in capturing the unaccustomed sense of idyll.

The music is more overt in setting the tone of particular scenes, but this itself only becomes evident upon second or third viewing. For its intended purpose – a one-off broadcast – Raymond Jones's score sits nicely behind the action, manipulating the viewer with short audial cues. There is menace for when Ascaris is lying in wait with his sword (merging nicely to harp playing in the village); epic danger for when the slave traders set off to the villa; dreaminess in contrast at the villa; then mournful tones when Ian and Barbara are being sold as slaves.

Perhaps the most curious use of incidental music – and the most significant in terms of the direction in which *The Romans* was to take **Doctor Who** – is that used for the killing of Maximus Pettulian: a mixture of light-stepping and sinister notes (surprisingly, not jarring), ending in an uplift sufficient to constitute... happiness? The balance is too subtle for allegations of comedy death, yet enough to suggest the murder is all according to plan: not Ascaris' but rather the **programme**'s. An old man has been done away with, we are reassured, but that was inevitable and indeed necessary if all is to end well.

Acting and Characterisation

One notable feature of Dennis Spooner's script for 'The Slave Traders' is that he finds four different pairings for the regular cast: the Doctor and Ian; Barbara and Vicki; Barbara and Ian; Vicki and the Doctor. Apart from one scene where they are all together (itself very good), the time travellers remain coupled. This works on several levels – affording the actors responsibility, variety, and space, both on set and within the dialogue – and allows all four to excel.

The Doctor begins his performance with some delighted hooting[150]. As much as the Doctor himself is on holiday, William Hartnell clearly is relishing the opportunity to lighten the mood. He still retains the Doctor's volatility – displaying mock irascibility when told he has eaten ants' eggs, building to genuine pique when his competence is questioned – but it is a softer version of the touchy old man of previous serials.

---

[150] From the sound of which, viewers of *The Dark Crystal* (1982) may struggle not to retcon as an attempt to channel both Mystic and Skeksis.

The Doctor's grandfatherly affection for Maureen O'Brien's Vicki is sweetly played, while Hartnell's slightly flustered demeanour when dealing with the Centurion is clearly that of his character and not, as in later serials, something that might be attributed to the actor himself. Whatever his reputation for fluffing lines, in 'The Slave Traders' William Hartnell is very much in control of his performance.

William Russell is similarly relaxed as Ian, who for a rare half episode is spared the task of dealing heroically with the worst the universe can throw at him. His domestic scenes with Barbara are quite enchanting, whereas if played by lesser actors the interaction could easily have come across merely as filler. Jacqueline Hill herself is exceptional, presenting first as an older sister figure to Vicki, then as a woman in a more-or-less romantic relationship, then as a history teacher expressing genuine despair at what fate awaits her at the hands of Roman slave traders.

Modern day **Doctor Who** has elevated the Doctor's companions to a new level of importance, whereas for many years in the 20th century they were sorely neglected. For those viewers who have watched only 21st-century **Who**, or who moved from one series to the next and laud this newfound empowerment, it is easy to forget that **Doctor Who** began life with companions as its **main characters**. Unsurprisingly, quality actors were cast in the roles; if ever anyone should doubt this, direct them to the subtlety of Barbara's expressions as she stands in the background and watches Vicki trying to buy fabric at the marketplace[151].

---

[151] Or, as Gary Gillatt notes in his review of the 2009 DVD release:

Vicki, of course, is the least developed of the regulars, but the month-long break in the plot plasters over her arrival and allows her an instant rapport with her three companions. Maureen O'Brien, 21 years old at the time, is very convincing in her portrayal of Vicki as a flighty teen. Dennis Spooner's script allowed Vicki to be impatient at the slowness of life at the villa, happily impertinent when pulling the Doctor up on his anachronistic use of French, yet genuinely disturbed when confronted with the body of Maximus Pettulian. In contrast with some later companions (who in fairness had less to work with), Maureen O'Brien is very natural in handling the changes in Vicki's demeanour.

Dennis Spooner's pairing of characters continued beyond the regular cast, most notably with the slave traders Sevcheria (Derek Sydney) and Didius (Nicholas Evans), but also then with the Doctor and the Centurion (Dennis Edwards). The latter two form an obvious double act, Hartnell playing the funny man and Edwards – in a similar way to Graham Chapman in many **Monty Python** skits – embodying the straight man with glorious, slightly embroidered rigidity. Sevcheria and Didius are perhaps less obviously a double act (think the Elizabethan Blackadder and Baldric sans any overt humour)[152], but the height difference speaks volumes and Derek Sydney has tremendous presence in a bored, stalking, superior way. Nicholas Evans, unfortunately, proves to be a weak link, but even

---

'Guest star Derek Francis may be the focus of the fruity farce in episode 3, but when he propositions Barbara – "Close your eyes, and Nero will give you a big surprise" – it's Hill's expert double-take that turns it into a thoroughly dirty joke.' (Gillatt, 'The Rescue and The Romans', *DWM* #406.)

[152] **Blackadder II** (1986).

his shortcomings might be put down to pre-empting the farce of 'Conspiracy'. His background acting is quite respectable while lurking behind Sevcheria at the marketplace; it is only when he tries with stilted lack of success to sheathe his sword that his character bombs out.

A few of the other roles are dubious – Margot Thomas seems unjustifiably sour as the stall holder; Edward Kelsey plays the slave buyer as being unhinged (which at least makes the point of life being cheap) – but there is only one that crosses into outright misgiving: Ascaris, as played by Barry Jackson (not that Jackson can be blamed as such). He plays an assassin of little intellect and questionable competence, and even when he does away with Maximus Pettulian – a frail, toothless old man who'd die if sneezed at – he uses a blunt-looking sword to make heavy, clumsy work of what could, with a knife, have been a straightforward throat-slitting.

None of this, however, is particularly reprehensible, especially if we make allowances for the cruelties of single-take filming. And let's remember: the only off note from either William Russell or Jacqueline Hill comes during the villa fight scene, when Barbara, in what presumably was envisaged as an accident within a melee, appears very deliberately to clobber Ian with an amphora!

The Story

'The Slave Traders' begins with the Doctor and company on holiday. There are several (quite long) scenes where the usual peril is entirely lacking. The *Radio Times* listing is almost criminally understated; yet, it is the very tranquillity of this new setting – the safety it offers – that brings intensity to the danger when it arrives.

And despite the prolonged moments of languor, it **does** come.

In the space of an episode that refrains from obvious cut-and-paste action, a surprising amount happens: a cliffhanger is resolved; a holiday is taken (allowing Vicki a smooth transition from token replacement for Susan to accepted TARDIS crew member); the setting is established (including the first historical peril of Rome: slavery); a musician is killed; the Doctor and company split up; Ian and Barbara are kidnapped by slavers; the Doctor impersonates the slain musician; Ian and Barbara are separated; and finally we reach a new cliffhanger in which the same assassin who killed Maximus Pettulian creeps, sword in hand, towards the room where the Doctor is practising his lyre...

And all this before Derek Francis makes his first appearance!

'All Roads Lead to Rome'

> 'Barbara is auctioned in the market square and Ian becomes a galley slave.'
>
> [*Radio Times* billing for 'All Roads Lead to Rome']

How to Resolve a Cliffhanger

Cliffhangers were the hallmark – some would say the bane – of many a weekly adventure serial, with the hero or heroine left dangling from a rocky outcrop, strapped to railway tracks, wired to a bomb or some other such peril, the escape from which usually entailed showing an edited version in the following week's recap. (For example, in week one the car's brakes fail and we see a close-up of the hero's face as the tyres crest the edge of the cliff. In week two there's a shot inserted of the hero jumping clear before the car ever got that far.)

The solution, in short, was usually a cheat; and while **Doctor Who** may have been less inclined than some programmes to fiddle the footage, it was often no less gratuitous in the solutions devised. In fact, many **Doctor Who** cliffhangers were not cliffhangers at all but rather end-of-shift whistle-blowing screams that proved, upon a week's reflection, to have been totally unwarranted. 1960s **Who** was not always much better, but in 'All Roads Lead to Rome' we see the previous week's peril play out to genuine resolution. Ascaris attacks the Doctor. Death is in the air! Granted, Barry Jackson hits his mark and then gives William Hartnell a second or two to react before swinging his sword[153], but nonetheless...

The significance of this opening scene should not be understated, for it is here as much as anywhere that *The Romans* successfully melds comedic elements with serious drama. The Doctor is struck at by a sword-wielding assassin. He blocks the blow with his lyre. At this point in the cliffhanger code we might well expect someone to intervene, but instead the Doctor – who, let us remember, in this first incarnation was a frail old man – reacts with great vigour, spurred into action and exclaiming: 'Ooh, so you want to fight, do you?'[154] He then hits Ascaris with a pot, wraps him in a blanket, blinds him with wine, brains him with an amphora, dodges his

---

[153] Barry Jackson, in *What Has 'The Romans' Ever Done For Us?* recalls:

> 'I remember going for him with a gladius – the little sword – and waiting for about four minutes while he turned round with his lyre, so I'm endlessly going, "Ahhh, ahhhhhh, ahhh... hurry up, ahhh..." you know, before he turns around.'

[154] The phrasing and delivery will seem uncannily familiar to viewers who grew up on **Monkey** (BBC, 1979-80).

sword swipes and judo-flips him to the floor! It is only **after** the Doctor has saved himself that Vicki arrives with a second amphora raised to strike, thereby prompting the cowed and whimpering Ascaris to throw himself out the second storey window.

The fight scene is wonderfully played, the music changing in tone from the quivering threat of Ascaris' approach, through sprightly baby elephant steps as the Doctor fights back, to jaunty spikes and crescendos as the assassin is beaten and then bested. Its true beauty, however, lies in the fact that the comedy is not 100% overt. The Doctor laughs off the attempt on his life, but the script and the performance make it unclear whether he is being truly frivolous or merely playing down the danger so as not to alarm Vicki. Raymond Jones' score can be interpreted in similar terms — is it highlighting the humour or mitigating against young viewers' apprehension? — and thus for one of the few times ever in **Doctor Who** we are presented with a serious cliffhanger, properly resolved... but only through dint of the serial's subtly employed comedy.

A similar dynamic can be seen at play when the Doctor and Vicki twice miss encountering (and no doubt saving) Barbara: firstly, at the slave auction, because the Doctor steers Vicki away from such unpleasantness; and secondly in the palace when Tavius calls for the Doctor to be brought to him but then changes his mind, unwilling to discuss murder and conspiracy in front of the new slave. In both instances the comedic staple of paths not-quite-crossed is juxtaposed with the very real dangers that Rome presents.

Direction, Script, Costume and Design

The Doctor's tussle with Ascaris was a triumph for all concerned:

actors, director, writer, composer, and fight arranger Peter Diamond. Christopher Barry's direction was in fact first-rate, and continued to be so throughout the episode. This is seen particularly in his depiction of the slave galley, which he establishes with stock footage before cutting to a well-matched interior set from Cusick. The storm and subsequent wrecking of the galley are quickly and astutely cut, and it is clear that Barry knows both what he needs to show and how long he can stay on any given shot while still holding the audience. The establishing model of Rome is relatively poor, but is on screen for only four seconds (across three cuts) and judiciously obfuscated both by documentary musical tones and by the zooming title: ROMA.

If Cusick had little money left for Rome in toto then let it be said that his sumptuous interpretation of Nero's palace – marble columns, patterned floors, numerous busts and statuary on plinths – goes a long way towards selling the Emperor's character. Daphne Dare was equally accommodating with Nero's costume: ornate robes with jewelled wristbands, garish finger rings and five (!) dangling necklaces, all topped with a bedazzling garland that to the modern eye smacks of metrosexual vanity.

Even before he speaks the emperor is grandiloquent, albeit with a regalia somewhat undermined by the large turkey drumstick he's clutching in one hand. It is this framing – again, the serious coupled with the slightly absurd – that allows Derek Francis to play Nero the way he does.

Acting and Characterisation

From the moment he speaks, Derek Francis has real presence, and while this star power does not manifest in a vacuum – in part it stems from the prominence of his being **written** as a major player – the acting quality is clear and its effect undeniable: William Hartnell is suddenly **challenged** for the lead role, and through that challenge is enabled himself to shine more brightly.

There is tension when Nero and the Doctor first meet. Cutting through the Doctor and Vicki's levity, the mood abruptly turns serious[155]. Within 30 seconds of Nero's entrance – sharply directed, with nine different camera shots – the emperor has butted horns with the Doctor and demanded that, in his guise as Maximus Pettulian, he play the lyre. What follows is a battle of wits. Appealing to Nero's vanity, the Doctor deftly sidesteps the command. Nero, however, wins out in a bit of comic business involving a stool, first resting his foot on it then holding his ground as the Doctor tries unsuccessfully to move in and replicate that same heroic stance. When Nero departs, the Doctor has won the first round… but is mildly nonplussed at being left with the drumstick.

The introduction of the show's major guest star is, in short, a triumph, its well-scripted exchange given extra vim by the gusto of Christopher Barry's direction. The Doctor and Vicki, as they do all episode, play beautifully off each other, while the prospect of further to-and-fro between the Doctor and Nero is, to say the least, more tantalising than the Emperor's half-chewed turkey.

In addition to Nero, two new characters are introduced in 'All Roads Lead to Rome'. The first of these is the galley slave Delos, played by

---

[155] Whether it be through scripting or happenstance, it is hard not to see this affably duelistic (to coin a homophone) encounter as mirroring that of Hartnell and Francis themselves.

Peter Diamond, with whom Ian is paired for much of the story's remainder. Diamond was hired primarily as a fight arranger – clearly a very good one – his acting being secondary in every sense. In fairness to him, however, it should be noted that Delos, like Ascaris, is dressed only in a sack (always difficult to act in), and is lumbered with a great deal of expository dialogue. His part is far from brilliant, yet not abysmal; a kind of poor man's Obelix to William Russell's Asterix.

The final newcomer, played by Michael Peake, is the slave buyer Tavius, a character invested with significant ambiguity. Short and balding, Tavius plays two long scenes with Barbara where it is unclear whether he is monastic and altruistic or leering and lascivious – an odd distinction not to be able to make, yet Peake's is a very nuanced performance, aided by his naturally expressive face, a deliberately equivocal script, and most notably (once looked for) an absence of the musical cues used elsewhere by Raymond Jones to shepherd viewers in the right direction[156]. This last is truly a masterstroke of characterisation, hiding the story's one key uncertainty on the silent flipside of the other players' more overt musical accompaniment. Having been inculcated to associate music with function, in the case of Tavius we are left in a vacuum.

Of the recurring characters, Derek Sydney's Sevcheria once again impresses as the amoral, sardonic slave trader, unpaired this

---

[156] Toby Hadoke has noted a similarly effective use of silence in 'The Dead Planet' (*The Daleks*, episode 1), which although scored by a different composer – Tristram Cary – was Christopher Barry's first contribution to **Doctor Who** (Shearman, Robert, and Toby Hadoke, *Running Through Corridors*, p17).

episode from his sidekick Didius (who doesn't feature). Jacqueline Hill is a pleasure to watch, her performance outshining those of her fellow regulars and imbuing Barbara with very real human emotions: compassion, worry, hope, anger, resignation, determination, and distrust. Although *The Romans* is best remembered as a comedy, its humour would be far less effective if not for Barbara's subplot (and to a lesser extent Ian's) and the serious manner in which this is both scripted and acted.

The Story

'All Roads Lead to Rome' passes very quickly, in part due to the quality of performances and in part because Dennis Spooner and Christopher Barry build rapidly from the foundations laid down in 'The Slave Traders'.

In the space of 23 minutes a cliffhanger is resoundingly resolved, Rome is revealed, Barbara is leered at – perhaps – and then sold, Nero makes his grand entrance, the Centurion from 'The Slave Traders' is found dead, and in the meantime Ian is consigned to a slave galley, shipwrecked, recaptured, and threatened in a new cliffhanger with being thrown to the lions!

Alongside the underwhelming Rome model these stock footage lions constitute the only slightly off note for the week, their threat being somewhat removed. Nevertheless, 'All Roads Lead to Rome' must go down as one of the most entertaining and accomplished of all William Hartnell episodes.

'Conspiracy'

'Dr Who gives a concert although he cannot play a note; and Nero's life is put in danger.'

The Story: Third Episode Run-Around?

In the 1970s and into the 1980s, when four-part stories were all the rage, a host of **Doctor Who** Script Editors, directors and Producers could be heard lamenting the troublesome third episode[157]: the one after the scenario had been established and the villain or monster revealed, yet before the Doctor could save the day, deal with the latest cataclysmic danger and toddle off back to the TARDIS; the episode, in short, where there was nothing much to do except run about the place and fill in 23 minutes.

Given its notoriety as the farce episode of **Doctor Who**, one might expect 'Conspiracy' to exemplify – perhaps even to have initiated – this tradition of frenetically treading water. It does no such thing.

Yes, Nero chases after Barbara; and yes, there is a considerable amount of comedic not-quite-meeting-up as the Doctor and Vicki roam separately throughout the palace, circumstances contriving always to keep them from encountering her. But there is so much more: Nero's wife Poppaea is introduced, as is the Emperor's official poisoner, Locusta; the intrigue of Tavius and the titular conspiracy is maintained; history itself is threatened as Vicki switches goblets and very nearly has Nero poisoned; the Doctor performs his Emperor's New Clothes lyre routine; and Barbara is finally reunited with Ian... at the Circus Maximus, where Nero is arranging to have the Doctor thrown to the lions. In a new cliffhanger Ian is forced to fight Delos and ends the episode on his knees, a sword pressed to the back of his neck.

---

[157] And still can be on a DVD commentaries.

'Conspiracy', then, is atypical not just in having farcical elements but also in avoiding what in later years would become **Doctor Who**'s third-episode syndrome. The farce is there – in memory it might dominate – yet without it the episode would still function. (Indeed, such is the amount of material packed into 'Conspiracy', it actually overruns quite badly[158].) However it might be judged, clearly the capering aspect was not added to the story merely to pass the time.

Directing and Scoring Nero's Carry-On

Right from the outset, 'Conspiracy' presents as if it will be something unique in the **Doctor Who** canon. Subsequent to the reprise of Ian contemplating lions, we cut to a scene of Nero walking towards camera, dictating an off-the-cuff composition to Tigilinus. Checking over the notation, he spots something amiss, scribbles an angry correction and storms off, breaking stride only long enough to smash his lyre over Tigilinus' head. The sequence is entirely without dialogue, and plays out to half-sinister, quarter-imperial, quarter-lampooning musical accompaniment.

This music is a precursor of the pure farce to come, returning and in fact ramping up to unabashed frivolity when Nero, with a call of, 'Yoo-hoo! I've been waiting for you. I'm coming after you...,' surprises Barbara outside Poppaea's chambers and gives prolonged chase after this latest, skittish object of his affections.

Many a long-running programme has at some point taken recourse to that scene, usually filmed quite statically, where the chaser pursues the chasee down a hallway and in and out of adjacent corridors, disappearing either stage left or stage right only to pop

---

158 26m 24s for the 25-minute slot.

up again from somewhere visually illogical[159]. Although this can be seen to an extent during Nero's pursuit of Barbara – when she eludes him at the far end of the corridor, he comes back, turns left, and is elated then to find her chasing **him** – Christopher Barry for the most part eschews such an approach, preferring instead to focus on the interruptions to Nero's libidinous sallying forth: first by Tigilinus; then by Vicki; then the Doctor. Barry cuts quickly within the scene, adding zest and pace to the comings and goings. His changes of camera angle, combined with Ray Cusick's false-perspective backdrops, turn what could have been a hackneyed bit of one-set pantomime into a genuine (if still preposterous) chase through the imperial palace.

The combination of music, movement, and quick cutting is taken up again in more enclosed surroundings when Nero follows Barbara to Poppaea's chambers and corners her there. Whatever one's opinion of farce, there's no denying that Christopher Barry and Raymond Jones pay due diligence to their rendition. Nero, for instance, could have made his entrance in one static shot. Instead, Barry shows him parting the curtains in the background behind Barbara, cuts to a two-second close-up of the emperor's peekaboo face and then back to the original shot as Nero sneaks up and grabs Barbara by her shoulders.

Whereas plenty of directors would have judged there to be too little reward for effort in the planning and coordination of such finicky

---

[159] For a striking example in 21st-century **Doctor Who** see David Tennant and Billie Piper's brief but frenetic appearance at the beginning of *Love & Monsters* (2006), discussed in Haringsma, Niki, *The Black Archive #28: Love & Monsters*.

live-edited camerawork, Barry clearly saw the benefit. Even where his direction can't quite keep the action looking plausible – such as when Barbara veers away from Nero but the latter carries on, blinkered and oblivious, to pull open a curtain revealing the Doctor – Barry pre-emptively has Jones plaster over the cracks. Such is the progression of notes from hot pursuit to surprised sting (and such is the fine line that farce must tread), the melding of directorial vision with musical score turns a might-have-flopped moment into the ridiculous but triumphant crescendo of a lusty pursuit gone astray.

More than a Smidgeon of Tigilinus

From the opening scene where he ends up wearing Nero's lyre, through to his ignominious expiry, Tigilinus presents as something of a cartoon character: he follows Nero around, trying unsuccessfully to fit the emperor with his crown; he slows down Nero's pursuit of Barbara with two separate bouts of overly assiduous robe-carrying; he cuts in on Nero when the emperor is puckering up to solicit a kiss from Barbara; and at last, in **Doctor Who**'s first ever comedy death[160], he drinks from Nero's poisoned chalice and drops, eyes rolling, from picture.

Actor Brian Proudfoot does an able job in the circumstances, but the part of Tigilinus is unforgiving. He is an unwanted distraction – like the intrusive sword in the Doctor's conversation with Nero, a forced and unnecessary bit of comic business – and we are left asking, 'Do we really need him?' In essence Tigilinus is little more

---

[160] More accurately, the first **confirmed** comedy death. The assassin Ascaris isn't seen again after diving out the window in 'All Roads Lead to Rome', and may well have perished. Both are non-speaking roles and leave the story with a musical flourish.

than a human prop that Derek Francis makes use of even while his character takes umbrage. And yet, the pussyfooting silent comedy forms a necessary piece of prefiguring, for if Tigilinus were not already established as the court jester, his death would be more shocking and Nero's glib reaction to it less amusing.

The Dallier at Large and the Indulgent Uncle

In the realms of gallows humour, Derek Francis' performance at the point of Tigilinus' demise must constitute a masterclass: the calculation in his eyes as it occurs to him to have Tigilinus drink the wine; the casual self-importance of body language in asserting 'you not me'; and finally his blithe indifference – the wonderful little shrug – at the loss of any life not his own. Nero's character is without doubt over the top, yet Francis brings a subtlety to his remit, anchoring the humour of his portrayal to the capricious real-life cruelty of the emperor.

A second anchor for Nero's excesses (both in plot and in tone) comes courtesy of the Doctor, who not only participates in the farce but also looks with what seems genuine fondness upon the emperor and his antics. The characterisation of the Doctor throughout 'Conspiracy' lends tacit approval to the goings on. Tigilinus dies, left at Nero's merciless whim while the Doctor hurries off, but so what? The Doctor has made it clear that the past must not be changed; so long as he and Vicki stay true to that maxim – which to the Doctor's mind they do – anything else that happens is just history, and ipso facto wholly appropriate. However licentious he might be, Nero must be saved from Vicki's interference. Whoever else then dies a result…? Well, that's none of their business.

The quandary of whether or not historical events can or should be altered crops up quite often in **Doctor Who**, but rarely with the insouciance of Vicki's almost poisoning of Nero. The Doctor's reaction when he finds out emphasises the importance of this one key tenet of time travel and yet, through contrast to his chuckling and hooting elsewhere, reaffirms that everything else is fair game. The outrageous comedy is acceptable because in the grand scheme of history it doesn't matter; the Doctor himself condones it.

And William Hartnell, let it be said, is in fine form throughout, seeming on the one hand to have been spurred on by Derek Francis' presence, while on the other to have been enjoying the more relaxed historical holiday setting. Much to his credit, Hartnell draws whatever humour is required from within the Doctor's character. The comedy of his performance comes not out of the blue, but rather from a tweaking – sometimes an exaggerating – of personality traits and tics that previously had been more dramatically in evidence.

A case in point: having been led with some reluctance into a clandestine conversation with Tavius, and having come out of it none the wiser, the Doctor levels a caustic pish-hiss at the retreating back of his wearisome and unintelligible would-be conspirator. It is a delightfully crabby reaction, and one that perfectly encapsulates the notion of an innately irascible time traveller mollified – but only within reason – by the diverting nature of his current surroundings.

'That strange young woman has been chasing me round all morning...'

'Conspiracy' is notorious for its farce, but what allows this to work is that while the first-billed actor spends much of the episode chortling and looking pleased with himself, and while the big-name guest star romps lasciviously about the palace, four actresses are giving very serious performances[161].

Jacqueline Hill may not look entirely at ease being chased after, yet she stays true to her character and in the less boisterous moments of Nero's wooing conveys perfectly the rigid, trapped helplessness of someone suffering from (to anticipate the concept) workplace harassment.

Maureen O'Brien provides something of a bridge between the episode's dramatic and comedic threads, but in all instances gives a very natural, very convincing performance. Vicki is a teenage girl from the far future, let loose in the imperial palace. Little wonder that she giggles at the emperor's pratfall, is disquieted by the notion of a court-sanctioned poisoner, or indeed that she casually tries to right the perceived injustice of a less important historical personage than Nero being slated for death. To Vicki it must all seem quite unreal – almost a dream – and O'Brien captures this beautifully.

Anne Tirard, who plays the stern-faced Locusta, is disproportionally memorable in what amounts to a relatively minor role. We are introduced to her with a portentous one-second close-up of her stony expression. Next time we see her she has befriended Vicki, although her severe appearance and the nature of her profession

---

[161] Derek Sydney's Sevcheria, promoted from slave master to gladiatorial impresario, helps also to weigh in against the levity, while William Russell is touchingly sombre in his limited screen time; nevertheless, it is the women who steal the show.

remain tellingly in contrast with her almost neighbourly willingness to chew the fat. Tirard does not overplay her part, so the audience, unlike with Tigilinus, is not anaesthetised against her fall. Locusta is severe-looking but not 'bad'. The sight of her being harangued and shoved and sent to her death by Poppaea thus comes as a shock – all the more so because we know Locusta's failure was due to Vicki's interference.

Kay Patrick as Poppaea is in fact the highlight of the episode: the measured superciliousness by which she can mollify Nero's bumptious pomposity even while looking down her nose at him; the heightened asperity of her disapproval when he takes a fancy to Barbara; the predatory authority she lets surface in Nero's absence; her simmering, woman-scorned disdain when she catches the emperor in flagrante; and finally her tyrannical rage at Locusta when the poisoning goes wrong. Poppaea's presence is the sumptuously costumed steel behind the roly-poly comedy facade. Without the strength of Kay Patrick's performance, the story would be in danger of collapse.

The Road Less Travelled, The Farce More Refined

'Conspiracy', for all its comic renown, is an episode balanced by astute direction and seriously good – if not always serious per se – acting. Nor is its humour entirely farcical. Yes, Dennis Spooner dropped in that flagrantly risqué suggestion: 'Now, close your eyes and Nero will give you a big surprise'; but there are other, more understated lines.

For instance:

LOCUSTA

So, you've arrived with the great Maximus Pettulian, have you? The court just cannot wait to hear him play, my dear.

VICKI

[Half to herself, aware the Doctor is no musician.]

They may have to.

Or when Nero is saved from drinking the poisoned wine:

[The Doctor and Vicki rush into the banqueting hall.]

DOCTOR

Caesar Nero, don't drink!

NERO

[Offscreen] Why not?

DOCTOR

[Approaching] I have every reason to believe that drink is poisoned.

[Nero, shocked, drapes an arm around Vicki for support.]

DOCTOR

Oh, ha-ha-hum. Yes, thank heavens I got to you in time.

NERO

My dear Maximus, you probably saved my life. If only I could lay my hands on whoever was responsible...

At which point Derek Francis directs a glance and a nod at Vicki, sublimely played to suggest that Nero is looking for a sympathetic understanding of his position. The dramatic irony of course is that he quite literally **does** have his hands on the culprit!

'Conspiracy' may constitute an audacious leap of faith into the realms of comedy – perhaps sometimes it goes too far – but this is just lovely.

'Inferno'

> 'Ian and Barbara are reunited, and the Doctor starts a fire.'
>
> [*Radio Times* billing for 'Inferno']

The Comedy Comes Crashing Down

From the outset of 'Inferno' it becomes clear that the comedy, so evident the previous week, has given way to the darker characterisation it helped disguise. From the reprise of Nero giving the thumbs down and commanding, 'Cut off his head!', the duel between Delos and Ian breaks out into an extended fight between them and the guards. All hint of frivolity is gone. The music is a straight mix of historical epic and dramatic action, while Nero, who had previously watched with the amused excitement of a child, now takes on the more cruel aspect of a boy who would pull the legs off insects.

When one of the guards is killed and falls at his feet, Nero berates the corpse – 'Get up, you coward, and fight! Get up; your Caesar commands it!' – and kicks it from the dais. The emperor is no longer the fat naughty fool of 'Conspiracy'. In the silence that ensues once Ian and Delos escape, his demeanour turns cold and deadly. The fun is well and truly over, and this change in mood is reflected quite exquisitely in the nervous fear shown by both

Barbara and Sevcheria (despite that the latter should be in no danger). They are tense; uncertain in Nero's presence. The emperor, we learn, is no mere blusterer or haughty buffoon; he is seriously unhinged.

'If you succeed, you will be rewarded,' an apprehensive Sevcheria is told; 'If you fail...' (Derek Francis quantifies the emperor's indifference with a supremely understated matter-of-fact hand gesture) '...you die.'

What has happened to the jolly farce of 'Conspiracy'? As Nero reverts to type (historically speaking), his cavorting hasn't just disappeared. It has been subverted; cast in a new light. Beneath the emperor's façade of overindulged tantrummer lurks the soul of a sociopath – perhaps even a psychopath – who lacks all sense of perspective and empathy. 'Give me your sword,' he commands the guard holding Barbara, then stabs viciously, drawing from Barbara what sounds like a cry of agony. This moment of directorial trickery (Nero has his back to the camera) sees instead the guard topple lifeless to the floor, whereupon Nero explains to Barbara, not with the heightened indifference afforded to Tigilinus' demise but rather with utter sincerity: 'He didn't fight hard enough.'

This is gallows humour at its darkest, and while Jacqueline Hill's reaction is **almost** that of someone rolling her eyes at the joke, her immersion in the role is sufficient to keep her performance true to Barbara's reality: she is in the presence of a very real, very dangerous and highly unpredictable madman.

All Roads Lead to the Dénouement

Christopher Barry mixes the vision judiciously and the musical cue carries over, linking Barbara's situation with that of Poppaea. Like

Barbara, the empress seems in danger of being overtaken by events. Though she will later recover her ruthless composure, for the moment she is vulnerable, uncertain of her position. Just as Barbara is left alone, her plight made somehow more serious by the emptiness of the corridors through which Nero once chased her, so too is Poppaea. Without her husband to rail against, she loses her conviction. There is an atmospheric foreboding – a sense of impending doom – and this is well marked by the subtle change in Kay Patrick's performance.

While Barbara and Poppaea are associated through means of Barry's direction, they are connected also within the script by their interactions with Tavius: Poppaea to demand his obedience and Barbara to seek his help. Tavius in fact is the bald screw holding the plot together, and though *The Romans* is very much a tale of character and wordplay, the dictates of television nevertheless obliged that its more-or-less-superfluous backstory at some point be told. It is during 'Inferno' that this happens.

Maximus Pettulian, it turns out, had journeyed from Corinth with the intention of murdering Nero. The centurion of 'The Slave Traders', learning of this but not informing the emperor, set out with Ascaris to dispose of Pettulian, then was himself killed by Pettulian's allies within Nero's court (who had been warned by Tavius). It seems improbable that the shambling lyre player of 'The Slave Traders' could have hoped to kill **anyone**, but such apparently was the conceit. Like Sevcheria's inexplicable promotion from slave trader to head of the imperial guard, it doesn't really need to make sense. Tavius divulges everything in a sharply directed information dump and then we move on, the whys and wherefores quickly forgotten.

Where Christopher Barry and Dennis Spooner were particularly shrewd was in using this mandatory bit of exposition to refocus attention on the Doctor, affording William Hartnell plenty of close-ups and having him come back down to earth from his gleeful, unconcerned Roman holiday. Hartnell is wholly convincing in switching between aspects of characterisation. Once alone with Vicki, the Doctor turns serious. Yes, he reverts to foolish banter in Nero's presence, but this is not the blithe wittering of earlier. Instead, we see the Doctor's sharpness of mind; the fierce intelligence that he can bring to bear when required. Like Barbara, Sevcheria and the audience, he is now aware of Nero's deranged machinations. Unlike those mentioned, however, he is neither disquieted nor afraid. He judges himself superior to the emperor, and sufficiently so that he may joke at Nero's expense.

While he is doing so, the notion is introduced of Rome burning.

To flammable characterisation is added the spark of wordplay. The Doctor strikes allusion after allusion, and as Nero's plans go up in flames so too does the episode catch light and blow quickly towards its conclusion. 'I'll have you both killed over and over again!' Nero rants. 'I'll have you tied to a stake in the middle of the arena, on an island with water all round and... and in the water there'll be alligators, and the water level will be raised and the alligators will get you!' This is a late gust of comedy, but if comedy was the life-breath of *The Romans* then it was also the accelerant by which drama smouldered and spread. Where the first three episodes struck out playfully, 'Inferno' is in deadly earnest.

Soon we have guards posted and Barbara watching in despair from a Juliet balcony. Ian and Delos sneak into the palace. Nero plots his grand arson, the source flame flickering lustily in the foreground. All of this is dramatically scored, and while Ian and Barbara escape, and likewise the Doctor and Vicki, Rome burns. Ray Cusick had run out of money by this point, so the great fire lacks a little visually[162]. Dramatically, however, it is the florescentia ab absurdum. As Nero plays his lyre, gleefully insane and abandoning himself to the conflagration, we realise *The Romans* wasn't really a comedy at all.

The overall effect is really very pleasing.

A Bit About Vicki

Maureen O'Brien gives another delightful performance, and with Christopher Barry's thoughtful direction establishes Vicki as a companion with great potential: not a like-for-like replacement for Susan but rather a whimsical, innocent teen whose carefree and wide-eyed approach to time travel seems perfectly tailored to match that of the programme's younger viewers.

Having listened to Tavius warn the Doctor he's to be thrown to the lions – a conversation she clearly understands given her subsequent appreciation of the Doctor's wordplay with Nero – Vicki nevertheless is dismayed when the Doctor tells her they must leave Rome immediately. She rubs at her arm where the guard's grip has bruised her, her expression suggesting both hurt resentment and a dissociation from the perilous reality of history. Later, when greeted

---

[162] Cusick, in *What Has 'The Romans' Ever Done For Us?*, laments: 'This was a last-minute request. Not only was it last-minute, there was nothing left in the kitty to pay for it. So it was a question of talking to the special effects people – Shawcraft Models – to see what they could do, you know, for a few pounds. I thought it looked awful. I nearly walked out of the studio in disgust.'

with the spectacle of Rome burning, she gasps, 'Doctor... look!', but what seems at first a horrified reaction turns out to be awe, wonder and excitement: 'My first real sight of history [...] Isn't it strange: to think that people will read about that in books for thousands and thousands of years and here am I sitting here, actually watching it!'

Vicki is bright and bubbly and will carry some of *The Romans'* levity into the more dour stories that follow. Maureen O'Brien, though at the beginning of her career, shows herself to be an actor of rather more talent than her appended fourth-billing might suggest. **Doctor Who** companions weren't always given much to do in the 20th-century serials, and increasingly made little of their screen time, yet O'Brien seems right at home alongside William Hartnell, and her background acting (for anyone who cares to pay attention) is nothing short of superb.

Ashes to Ashes, Farce to Farce

'Inferno' reaches its dramatic ending five minutes before the credits roll. What follows is an aesthetically pleasing bit of closure as first Ian and Barbara then Vicki and the Doctor return to the villa of 'The Slave Traders', both pairings still unaware of how near their paths came to crossing in Rome. Barbara and Ian have what can only be taken as a lovers' playful tiff, then we're back to tranquillity and birdsong and Ian expounding: 'Oh, tempera. Oh, mores.' (As he had done in 'The Slave Traders'.) The story has come full circle, and with one last musical nod to the might of Imperial Rome, the erstwhile schoolteachers follow after Vicki and the Doctor to the crookedly parked TARDIS and depart.

Even this is not the end. As the Doctor busies himself at the controls, Barbara concedes that the holiday is over: 'Oh well. Much as I like these clothes, I really think we ought to change into something a little more practical.' And Vicki rather sombrely agrees: 'Yes, you're right.' It's more than tempting to see this as a metatextual pronouncement on *The Romans* itself, Dennis Spooner pre-empting a negative opinion poll. As Barbara and Vicki go to change, the background hum of the TARDIS takes on a sinister hiss and the Doctor draws Ian into his worried confidence. A new cliffhanger manifests. Science fiction peril! 'Next Episode: THE WEB PLANET'.

For all its brilliance, the experiment in historical comedy is tied off and left behind, as though it never happened.

We know it did, of course. In 2008 we had it confirmed in *The Fires of Pompeii*. But in 1965 the **Doctor Who** production team left itself with (im)plausible deniability:

'Oh well,' Barbara concedes. (The Doctor, having plugged up Ian's attempt to tell the story, has gone off with Vicki.) 'Even if we had told them, I don't think they'd have believed us.'

'No,' Ian admits. '[They'd have] said we were dreaming.'

But what an inspired dream it was.

BIBLIOGRAPHY

Books

Asimov, Isaac, *The Naked Sun*. 1957. Grafton, 1960. ISBN 9780586010167.

Babington, Bruce, and Peter William Evans, *Biblical Epics: Sacred Narrative in the Hollywood Cinema*. Manchester University Press, 1993. ISBN 9780719040306.

Cassius Dio, *Roman History*. CE 222. Herbert B. Foster, trans, Loeb, 1914-27.

Champlin, Edward, *Nero*. Cambridge, Harvard University Press, 2009. ISBN 9780674029361.

Chapman, James, *Inside the TARDIS: The Worlds of Doctor Who – A Cultural History*. London, IB Tauris, 2006. ISBN 9781845111632.

Corbeill, Anthony, *Nature Embodied: Gesture in Ancient Rome*. Princeton, Princeton University Press, 2004. ISBN 9780691074948.

Cotton, Donald, *Doctor Who: The Myth Makers*. **The Target Doctor Who Library** #97. London, WH Allen, 1985. ISBN 9780426201701.

Cotton, Donald, *Doctor Who: The Romans*. **The Target Doctor Who Library** #120. London, WH Allen, 1987. ISBN 9780426202882.

Deutsch, David, *The Beginning of Infinity: Explanations that Transform the World*. Viking, 2011. ISBN 9780670022755.

Driscoll, Paul, *Doctor Who (1996)*. **The Black Archive** #25. Edinburgh, Obverse Books, 2018. ISBN 9781909031791.

Evans, Judith, *Feminist Theory Today: An Introduction to Second-*

Wave Feminism. London, Sage, 1995. ISBN 9780803984782.

Fisher, David, *Doctor Who: The Leisure Hive*. **The Target Doctor Who Library** #39, 1982. ISBN 9780426201477.

Friedan, Betty, *The Feminine Mystique*. RS Means Company, 1964. ISBN 9780393084361.

Gold, Barbara K, and John F. Donahue, eds, *Roman Dining: A Special Issue of American Journal of Philology*. JHU Press, 2005. ISBN 9780801882029.

Roller, Matthew, 'Posture and Sex in the Roman *Convivium*'.

Goscinny, René, and Albert Uderzo, *Asterix the Gladiator (Astérix gladiateur)*. 1962. Anthea Bell and Derek Hockridge, trans, London, Hodder Dargaud, 1969. ISBN 0340104791.

Graves, Robert, *I, Claudius*. Arthur Barker, 1934. ISBN 9780141188591.

Graves, Robert, *Claudius the God*. Harrison Smith & Robert Haas, 1935. ISBN 9780141188607.

Gribbin, John, *Computing with Quantum Cats: From Colossus to Qubits*. Bantam, 2013. ISBN 9780593071144.

Griffin, Miriam T, *Nero: The End of a Dynasty*. 1984. London, Batsford, 1987. ISBN 9780713444657.

Haining, Peter, *The Doctor Who File*. London, WH Allen, 1986. ISBN 0491038135.

Pertwee, Jon, 'A Dandy Suit and Action Routes'.

Spooner, Dennis, 'The Secret of Writing for **Doctor Who**'.

Haringsma, Niki, *Love & Monsters*. **The Black Archive** #28. Edinburgh, Obverse Books, 2019. ISBN: 9781909031791.

Higgins, Patrick, *Heterosexual Dictatorship: Male Homosexuality in Postwar Britain*. London, Trafalgar Square, 1997. ISBN 9781857023558.

Hornblower, Simon, and Antony Spawforth, eds, *The Oxford Classical Dictionary* (Third Edition, Revised). New York, Oxford University Press, 2003. ISBN 9780198606419.

Howe, David J, and Stephen James Walker, *The Television Companion: The Unofficial and Unauthorised Guide to Doctor Who, Volume One*. UK, Telos Publishing, 2013. ISBN 9781845830762.

Kamm, Juergen, and Birgit Neumann, eds, *British TV Comedies: Cultural Concepts, Contexts and Controversies*. Palgrave MacMillan, 2014. ISBN 9781349555185.

Kilborn, Richard, 'A Golden Age of British Sitcom? **Hancock's Half Hour** and **Steptoe and Son**'.

Levy, Shawn, *Ready, Steady, Go! Swinging London and the Invention of Cool*. 2002. Sydney, Fourth Estate, 2014. ISBN 9780007375752.

Marwick, Arthur, *The Sixties: Cultural Revolution in Britain, France, Italy and the United States c.1958-1974*. Oxford, Oxford University Press, 1998. ISBN97801992100221.

Matyszak, Philip, *Ancient Rome on Five Denarii a Day*. 2007. London, Thames & Hudson, 2010. ISBN 9780500051474.

McLeod, Hugh, *The Religious Crisis of the 1960s*. Oxford, Oxford University Press, 2007. ISBN 9780199298259.

Miles, Lawrence and Tat Wood, *About Time 5: The Unauthorized*

Guide to Doctor Who, 1980-1984, Seasons 18 to 21. 2004. Des Moines, Mad Norwegian Press, 2010. ISBN 9780975944646.

Myles, LM, *The Ambassadors of Death*. **The Black Archive** #3. Edinburgh, Obverse Books, 2016. ISBN 9781909031395.

Orthia, Lindy, ed, *Doctor Who and Race*. Bristol, Intellect, 2013. ISBN 9781783200368.

> Fly, Fire, 'The White Doctor'.

> Hernandez, Mike, '"You Can't Just Change What I Look Like Without Consulting Me!": The Shifting Racial Identity of the Doctor'.

Pixley, Andrew, *The Goodies: Super Chaps Three*. Dudley, Kaleidoscope, 2010. ISBN 9781900203401.

Preuss, Julius, *Biblical and Talmudic Medicine*. Fred Rosner, trans, New York, Sanhedrin Press, 1978. ISBN 9781568211343.

Price, Simon, *Rituals and Power: The Roman Imperial Cult in Asia Minor*. Cambridge, Cambridge University Press, 1984. ISBN 9780521259037.

Robinson, John AT, *Honest to God*. London, Westminster John Knox Press, 1963. ISBN 9780664244653.

Sandifer, Elizabeth, *TARDIS Eruditorum I: William Hartnell*. Createspace, 2011. ISBN 9781467951586.

Saward, Eric, *Doctor Who: Slipback*. **The Target Doctor Who Library**, 1986. ISBN 9780426202635.

Shearman, Robert, and Toby Hadoke, *Running Through Corridors: Rob and Toby's Marathon Watch of* **Doctor Who**, *Volume 1: The*

60s. 2010. Des Moines, Mad Norwegian Press, 2011. ISBN 9781935234067.

Suetonius, *The Twelve Caesars*. CE 121. J. C. Wolfe, trans, Loeb, 1914.

Tacitus, *Annals*. CE 115-120. John Jackson, trans, Loeb, 1931-37.

Thompson, Ben, ed, *Ban this Filth! Letters from the Mary Whitehouse Archive*. London, Faber and Faber, 2012. ISBN 9780571281497.

Tulloch, John, and Manuel Alvarado, *Doctor Who: The Unfolding Text*. New York, St. Martin's Press, 1983. ISBN 9780312214804.

Walker, Stephen James, *Talkback: The Unofficial and Unauthorised Doctor Who Interview Book; Volume One: The Sixties*. Surrey, Telos, 2006. ISBN 9781845830067.

'Interview: Dennis Spooner – Story Editor, Writer'.

Wood, Tat, and Lawrence Miles, *About Time 1: The Unauthorized Guide to Doctor Who, 1963-1966, Seasons 1 to 3*. 2006. Des Moines, Mad Norwegian Press, 2009. ISBN 9780975944606.

Wood, Tat, *About Time 6: The Unauthorized Guide to Doctor Who, 1985-1989, Seasons 22 to 26*. 2007. Des Moines, Mad Norwegian Press, 2011. ISBN 9780975944657.

Windschuttle, Keith, *The Killing of History: How Literary Critics and Social Theorists are Murdering our Past* (Revised Edition). 1996. San Francisco, Encounter Books, 2000. ISBN 9781893554120.

Wolfenden, John, *Report: Committee on Homosexual Offences and Prostitution*. London, HM Stationery Office, 1957.

Periodicals

Doctor Who Magazine (DWM). Marvel UK, Panini, BBC, 1979-.

>Gillatt, Gary, 'The Rescue and The Romans'. DWM #406, April 2009.

>Pixley, Andrew, 'The Romans'. DWM #251, May 1997.

Doctor Who: An Adventure in Space and Time #M: *The Romans.*

>Mount, Paul, 'Story Review'.

>Peel, John, 'Character Profiles'.

Edwards, Jacob, 'In the Shadow of Slartibartfast: Donald Cotton and *Doctor Who*'s Other Comedic Trilogy'. *Theaker's Quarterly* 37, summer 2011.

Pixley, Andrew. 'The Romans'. *Doctor Who: The Complete History* Volume #4. December 2017.

Television

The Benny Hill Show. BBC/ATV, 1955-67.

Blackadder. BBC, 1983-89.

Class. BBC, 2016.

Doctor Who. BBC, 1963-

>*The Awakening*. DVD, 2011.

>*The Crusade*. VHS, 1999.

>*The Chase*. DVD, 2010.

>>Commentary, Richard Martin, Maureen O'Brien, Peter Purves, William Russell.

The Power of the Daleks.

> Commentary, Michael Briant, Derek Dodd, Toby Hadoke, Anneke Wills.

The Romans. DVD, 2009.

> Commentary, Christopher Barry, Nick Evans, Toby Hadoke, Barry Jackson, William Russell.

> What Has 'The Romans' Ever Done For Us?

Vengeance on Varos. DVD, 2001.

> Commentary, Colin Baker, Nicola Bryant, Nabil Shaban.

The Epic That Never Was. BBC, 1965.

The Goodies. BBC, 1970-80.

> *Rome Antics.* 1975.

Hancock's Half Hour. BBC, 1956-61.

The Hitchhiker's Guide to the Galaxy. BBC, 1981.

I, Claudius. BBC, 1976.

> *Old King Log.*

Monty Python's Flying Circus. BBC, 1969-74.

Red Dwarf. BBC, 1988-99.

Ring-a-Ding-Ding. BBC, 1964.

Saiiyūki; aka **Journey to the West.** NTV, 1978-80.

Steptoe and Son. BBC, 1962-65.

The Young Ones. BBC, 1982-84.

Film

Henson, Jim, and Frank Oz, dirs, *The Dark Crystal*. Universal Pictures, 1982.

Kubrick, Stanley, dir, *Dr Strangelove*. Columbia Pictures, 1964.

Landis, John, dir, *The Blues Brothers*. Universal Pictures, 1980.

LeRoy, Mervyn, dir, *Quo Vadis*. Metro-Goldwyn-Mayer, 1951.

Lester, Richard, dir, *A Funny Thing Happened on the Way to the Forum*. United Artists, 1966.

Mankiewicz, Joseph L., dir, *Cleopatra*. 20th Century Fox, 1963.

Mann, Anthony, dir, *The Fall of the Roman Empire*. Paramount Pictures, 1964.

Scott, Ridley, dir, *Gladiator*. DreamWorks Pictures, 2000.

Thomas, Gerald, dir, *Carry On Cleo*. Anglo-Amalgamated, 1964.

Stage Plays

Sondheim, Stephen, Burt Shevelove and Larry Gelbart, *A Funny Thing Happened on the Way to the Forum*. 1962.

Radio

Doctor Who: *Slipback*. BBC, 1985.

The Goon Show. BBC, 1951-60.

Hancock's Half Hour. BBC, 1955-59.

Web

BBC Genome Project: Radio Times 1923-2009. https://genome.ch.bbc.co.uk/. Accessed 30 January 2019.

BBC News, 'Doctor Who's first Producer dies'. BBC News, 23 November 2007. http://news.bbc.co.uk/2/hi/entertainment/7109538.stm. Accessed 30 January 2019.

'David Whitaker (1970s)'. 23 October 2009. https://drwhointerviews.wordpress.com/2009/10/23/david-whitaker-1970s/. Accessed 30 January 2019.

Doctor Who Cuttings Archive. http://cuttingsarchive.org/index.php/Main_Page. Accessed 30 January 2019.

Doctor Who: *Scream of the Shalka*. Webcast. BBC, 2003. http://www.bbc.co.uk/doctorwho/classic/webcasts/shalka/. Accessed 30 January 2019.

'Keeping the Children Happy and Informed'. *The Times*, 23 January 1965. http://cuttingsarchive.org/index.php/Keeping_the_Children_Happy_and_Informed. Accessed 30 January 2019.

'The Leisure Hive'. *Whotopia*. http://www.whotopia.co.uk/scripts/story.asp?lngTVStoryID=110. Accessed 30 January 2019.

'Land of Make Believe'. *I'll Explain Later* #27, 15 October 2017. https://www.illexplainlater.com/post/166422653503/episode-27-land-of-make-believe. Accessed 30 January 2019.

'The Romans'. *BroaDWcast*. http://gallifreybase.com/w/index.php/The_Romans. Accessed 30 January 2019.

'*The Romans*'. *Doctor Who Target Book Club* #12, 24 June 2017. https://soundcloud.com/doctorwhotargetbookclubpodcast/ep-12-the-romans. Accessed 30 January 2019.

Aggas, James, '**Doctor Who** Retro Review: *The Romans* (First Doctor Story)'. *Doctor Who Watch*, April 2018. https://doctorwhowatch.com/2018/04/18/retro-review-romans/. Accessed 30 January 2019.

Clark, Laurence, 'Disabling Comedy: "Only When We Laugh!"'. Conference Paper, 2003. https://disability-studies.leeds.ac.uk/wp-content/uploads/sites/40/library/Clark-Laurence-clarke-on-comedy.pdf. Accessed 30 January 2019.

Duignan, Brian, 'Postmodernism'. 10 June 2009, revised 18 October 2018. https://www.britannica.com/topic/postmodernism-philosophy. Accessed 30 January 2019.

Fabry, Merrill, 'Where Does the "Thumbs-Up" Gesture Really Come From?'. *TIME*, 25 October 2017. http://time.com/4984728/thumbs-up-thumbs-down-history/. Accessed 30 January 2019.

Gillatt, Gary, 'The Rescue and The Romans'. *Squabbling Rubber*, 16 July 2011. https://gillatt.wordpress.com/2011/07/16/the-rescue-and-the-romans/. Accessed 30 January 2019.

Holstrom, John, 'I Can See Only the Wooden Charmlessness of the Adventurers'. *New Statesman*, 16 April 1965. http://cuttingsarchive.org/index.php/I_can_see_only_the_wooden_charmlessness_of_the_adventurers. Accessed 30 January 2019.

Lodder, B, 'Are They Monsters or Entertainment? The Position of the Disabled in Ancient Rome' (Masters Thesis). Leiden, Leiden University, 2017. https://openaccess.leidenuniv.nl/bitstream/handle/1887/53279/The%20position%20of%20the%20disabled%20in%20the%20Roman%20Empire.pdf?sequence=1. Accessed 30 January 2019.

Rovito, Maria R, *Disability and Mental Illness in 1960s Countercultural Literature* (Honours Thesis). Pennsylvania, Millersville University, 2016. http://www.academia.edu/29923283/Disability_and_Mental_Illness_in_1960s_Counterculture_Literature. Accessed 30 January 2019.

Webber, CE, and Sydney Newman, '"Dr Who" – General Notes on Background and Approach'. BBC, circa 1963. http://www.bbc.co.uk/archive/doctorwho/6403.shtml. Accessed 30 January 2019.

Wilson, Ralph F, 'Early Christian Symbols of the Ancient Church from the Catacombs'. *JesusWalk*. http://www.jesuswalk.com/christian-symbols/. Accessed 30 January 2019.

BIOGRAPHY

Jacob Edwards grew up with the starburst of 1980s **Doctor Who** and the psychedelic swirl and time tunnels of 1970s repeats. Although a fan of the programme – both classic and new series – he does not consider himself a Whovian. (He rarely re-watches episodes and can't even recognise Pat Gorman.) Nonetheless, he would like one day to write for **Doctor Who** or its spin-offs. It's up there on his bucket list alongside learning the harmonica and jamming with the Blues Brothers.

Jacob completed a BA in English and an MA in Ancient History at the University of Queensland. He writes creative and academic non-fiction, short stories, reviews and poetry, and has appeared in journals, magazines and anthologies in Australia, New Zealand, England, Canada and the US. He edited #45 and #55 of the *Andromeda Spaceways Inflight Magazine*, and writes YA fiction under a well-guarded pseudonym.

When not indulging his nostalgia for 80s synthpop, Jacob may be found online at www.jacobedwards.id.au or salvaging 42 word reviews at www.derelictspacesheep.com.

Coming Soon

The Black Archive #33: Horror of Fang Rock by Matthew Guerrieri

The Black Archive #34: Battlefield by Philip Purser-Hallard

The Black Archive #35: Timelash by Phil Pascoe

The Black Archive #36: Listen by Dewi Small

The Black Archive #37: Kerblam! by Naomi Jacobs and Thomas Rodebaugh

The Black Archive #38: The Underwater Menace by James Cooray Smith

The Black Archive #39: The Sound of Drums / Last of the Time Lords by James Mortimer

The Black Archive #40: The Silurians by Robert Smith?

The Black Archive #41: Vengeance on Varos by Jonathan Dennis

The Black Archive #42: The Rings of Akhaten by William Shaw

The Black Archive #43: The Robots of Death by Fiona Moore

The Black Archive #44: The Pandorica Opens / The Big Bang by Philip Bates

The Black Archive #45: The Unquiet Dead by Erin Horáková

The Black Archive #46: The Awakening by David Powell

The Black Archive #47: The Stones of Blood by Katrin Thier

The Black Archive #48: The Tenth Planet by Michael Seely

The Black Archive #49: Arachnids in the UK by Samuel Maleski

The Black Archive #50: The Day of the Doctor by Alasdair Stuart

The Black Archive #50A: The Night of the Doctor by James Cooray Smith